TUNISIA
The Politics of
Modernization

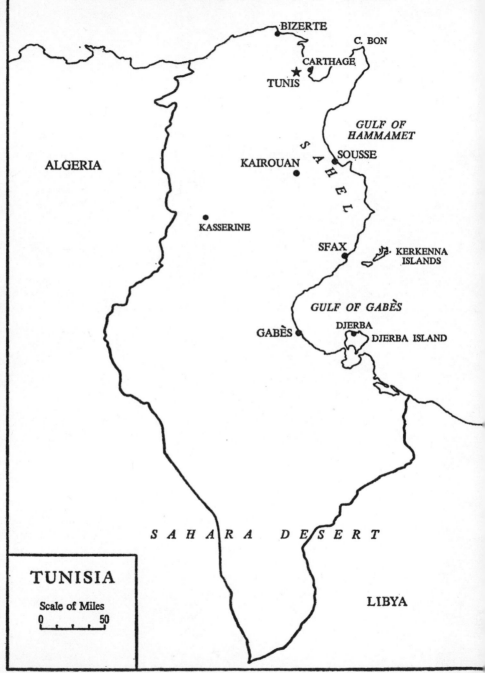

MEDITERRANEAN SEA

BIZERTE

C. BON

CARTHAGE

★
TUNIS

GULF OF
HAMMAMET

ALGERIA

S
A
H
E
L

KAIROUAN

SOUSSE

KASSERINE

SFAX

KERKENNA
ISLANDS

GULF OF GABÈS

GABÈS

DJERBA

DJERBA ISLAND

SAHARA DESERT

LIBYA

TUNISIA

Scale of Miles

0   50

TUNISIA

The Politics of Modernization

By **CHARLES A. MICAUD**

WITH Leon Carl Brown
AND Clement Henry Moore

FREDERICK A. PRAEGER, *Publisher*
New York · London

FREDERICK A. PRAEGER, PUBLISHER
64 UNIVERSITY PLACE, NEW YORK 3, N.Y., U.S.A.
77-79 CHARLOTTE STREET, LONDON W. 1, ENGLAND

Published in the United States of America in 1964
by Frederick A. Praeger, Inc., Publisher

© 1964 by Frederick A. Praeger, Inc.
Library of Congress Catalog Card Number: 64-13384

Printed in the United States of America

Prefatory Note

The three contributors to this book found themselves in Tunisia in 1960 and 1961. Both Leon Carl Brown and Clement H. Moore had received grants from the Ford Foundation, while I was employed at the ICA mission in Tunis as Higher Education Adviser. Since we were doing research in related fields, the idea of a joint undertaking on the theme of modernization followed quite naturally. Our group was unofficially joined by a young economist who has asked to remain anonymous; thanks to him, I dared venture on not too familiar ground. I am grateful to him as well as to my two collaborators for their patient and self-denying efforts in presenting an integrated book.

We wish to express our appreciation to our Tunisian friends in all walks of life for their spontaneous and generous help. So many of them gave us information and guidance that their contributions will have to remain anonymous.

At the risk of shocking certain conservative scholars, we have decided to solve the thorny problem of transliteration by adopting the spelling consistently used by the Tunisians in their publications in the French language.

C. A. MICAUD

Denver
December, 1963

Contents

Introduction

Of the new countries that in the past ten years have expanded the rolls of the United Nations, Tunisia is one of the smallest. Its area, which is slightly greater than that of New York State, consists for the most part of desert or arid steppe. Except for possible oil deposits, the country has few exploitable natural resources. Tunisia's 4 million inhabitants should be content to expect either a low rate of economic growth or perennial dependence upon massive foreign assistance.

Yet unlike most other new countries, Tunisia has adapted itself relatively painlessly to the challenges of the modern world. It offers a pattern of social development and a set of political institutions that, so far, seem to be meeting the task of modernization without sacrificing basic human values for totalitarian "short cuts." In many respects, the nation has become a model for developing states, and as such, it has been a favored recipient of American aid.

The specific importance of the Tunisian experience is that the pattern of development there helps clarify the entire process of modernization. A modern society cannot be defined only in terms of its technology or its social and political structures if the definition is to capture all aspects of the achievements for which the new countries are striving. Broad definitions are wiser: "Modernity is an opening up of the creative powers of ordinary people; it involves an appreciation of their rights and potentialities as individuals, of their capacities for expression, for happiness, for knowledge."[1] Modern society cannot restrict itself to gratifying rational needs; if it is not to be ill and fall short of its potentialities for growth, it must also, like the mature individual, be internally free and at peace with itself.

Modernization does, however, involve certain economic, social, and political changes, which can be summed up as follows: (1)

The authority of the *ancien régime* gives way to the rule of the people and, ideally, to the doctrine that they are equal before the law to which they individually consent. (2) The old social units, such as the family, village, or tribe, become subordinated to a national community; they are replaced as agents of social integration by new voluntary organizations, such as trade unions and political parties. (3) An old elite based on birth either dies out or becomes assimilated into a new elite based on achievement and education. (4) Traditional values are to a large extent undermined by a new faith—essentially the belief in material progress through the efficient use of human beings and technical innovations for maximum production. The new elite, and later the masses, demand jobs, an equitable distribution of wealth, constantly rising living standards, and ever-expanding social services.

Modernization—always a difficult process—faces more risks today than ever before. Societies are expected to change at a pace that may endanger the internal stability of even the most adaptable group. Furthermore, modernism is apt to be primarily a set of standards imposed upon a society by a small, and often confused, indigenous elite. When a young country copies a revolution that succeeded elsewhere, the new hybrid society may have a feeling of dependence upon the external stimulus or a sense of alienation from traditional values. Through a defense mechanism not unknown in Central and Eastern Europe in the nineteenth century, the newly independent people may borrow techniques only, while continuing to assert the excellence of their native culture, and hence suffer from a basic unresolved contradiction. Another risk is that authoritarian short cuts to technological advance may prove irresistible, although they subvert modernity's fundamental principle—the liberation of the people's creativity. Another danger threatens all uneven efforts at modernization: Traditional structures may disintegrate before new voluntary organizations learn to act as organs of social integration, or old values may be lost before new syntheses are achieved. Finally, mass expectations are likely to outrun production and threaten political stability; new governments may sometimes be unable to reconcile the need for greater production with that for adequate social services.

Clearly, the problem of modernization must be conscious and political; it requires social engineering, so far as modern man is capable of gauging and channeling social currents. It is necessary to try to understand the often conflicting forces within the society and bring them into accord with the aims of a modern state. The task is primarily political because it requires the consent, whenever feasible, of the people of the traditional society.

The Tunisian experience suggests a broad hypothesis that is probably relevant to most new countries: To the extent that modernization is a conscious and political process—which has been largely the case in Tunisia—its success seems to require that modern values be fully assimilated by as broad an elite as possible and that this elite be capable of effective action. In order to share its purposes with the people, the elite must act within the context of a mass movement, which it must organize. The mass movement may then serve as the embryo of the modern national community it is to forge. Furthermore, once the elite attains power, it must combine caution with innovation during the phase of consolidation of the new nation-state. It must avoid policies that would harm its cohesion and the ability of the people to comprehend and follow—even if this course seems to entail forfeiting maximum economic growth, at least in the immediate future.

This study of Tunisian modernization is divided into three parts. Part I is an analysis of the impact of the French colonization and of how and why Tunisian society—and, more precisely, its intellectual elite—responded as it did. Before the establishment of the French Protectorate in 1881, Tunisia was a state with centuries of tradition and a relatively homogeneous, viable society. The task of building a modern national community was, therefore, less difficult than in most other new countries. French rule encouraged the entry of a large European minority, which stimulated modernization yet was not large enough to constitute a serious threat to Tunisia's national identity. In response to the colonial situation, Tunisia seems to have reacted according to an "ideal" pattern of development that may be considered applicable to all transitional societies. A broad new elite eventually emerged from a relatively narrow base; it had assimilated modern values thoroughly and could act effectively within a mass movement for independence.

The focus of Part II is the political system as it has evolved since 1934, with the creation of the Neo-Destour, which became Tunisia's key instrument of modernization. What is today virtually a single-party system could perhaps have developed only out of the particular colonial situation that gave rise to it. It may be argued that in Tunisia, as in many other countries, the single party has for the most part been a valuable institution—indeed essential for modernization. The Neo-Destour Party enjoys a quasi monopoly of political power; nevertheless, although it does not operate in every respect along democratic lines, it is far from being a totalitarian party. It fulfills the two key functions of maintaining national cohesion and mobilizing the people along national and modernist lines while exercising a minimum of constraint and allowing a reasonable amount of discussion. The Neo-Destour, of course, cannot be analyzed without reference to its founder and hero, Habib Bourguiba, and though predictions can be attempted, only the future can tell if he is its only *raison d'être*.

Part III is an evaluation of the social and economic changes since independence was gained in 1956. Although as late as 1961 the economic results appeared meager, the society was undergoing a fundamental transformation through far-reaching reforms. Modernism as a state of mind was being effectively disseminated throughout the society. The usual Marxist or liberal categorizations do not suffice to explain either Tunisia's past or future course; one must seek explanations elsewhere. Above all, one must recognize that a deliberate effort was made at national consolidation, which is itself an intrinsic aspect of modernization, and which was made more urgent by Tunisia's involvement in the Algerian War. The Ten-Year Plan launched in 1961 and "Neo-Destourian Socialism," if somewhat too ambitious from an economic view, represent a conscious attempt at reconciling the social and economic facets of development.

Tunisia's pattern of modernization, of course, is still unfolding and therefore cannot be characterized with any degree of absoluteness. It should be stated at the outset that Tunisia is not yet a modern, democratic country. Nor is it certain that the young nation will carry out its experiment in long-range planning without sacrificing some of its commitments to liberal democratic values. But so far, Tunisia has been successful in carrying out the three major tasks of modernization that are the preconditions for rapid economic growth. It has succeeded in maintaining national cohesion, in mobilizing and educating the masses, and in transforming values and structures—without losing sight of the ultimate goal of modernization, the liberation of man. This accomplishment invites some degree of optimism about the future of the young nation. All this makes Tunisia the ideal vehicle for a case study of the politics of modernization.

I. Stages in the Process of Change

LEON CARL BROWN

1. Stages in the Process of Change: A Theoretical Model

What makes a country ready to undertake a program of modernization and rapid economic development? Certainly one of the most important factors is a psychological and intellectual commitment to change—an attitude which originates with the ruling elite but which must also strike a responsive chord in the masses. It is not enough that a few young men from a conservative, self-contained society have the opportunity to see and be impressed by a modern, dynamic society with entirely alien values. Although the program and detailed planning of economic development must come from the top, failure is inevitable unless there is popular receptivity.

Neither the elite nor the Tunisian masses were committed to change a hundred years ago. Rather, an evolution that in Western civilization took more than three centuries—from the Renaissance to the Industrial Revolution—has been telescoped in Tunisia into a few generations.

To the historian, the Tunisian case is part of the larger problem of understanding and interpreting what is usually called "the Western impact on the non-Western world." Until the nineteenth century, Tunisia, like most of the non-Western world, was theocentric, oriented toward the past, and hostile to change. But again like most of the non-Western world, it changed radically under the impact of an aggressive, dynamic Western society —an impact that involved either outright colonization or relentless pressure in other forms. What distinguishes Tunisia from other non-Western countries that started the process of development at about the same time, and from roughly the same level, is that it has made a more effective ideological adjustment to modern patterns.

To determine the reasons for this dynamic adjustment, it is necessary to trace the main currents of ideological change in Tunisia from the period just before the establishment of the French Protectorate, in 1881, until the mid-1930's, when the Neo-Destour was firmly established, not only as a political party but also as an ideological movement. This will not be a summary history of the period but rather a schematic attempt to isolate the most important factors in the Tunisian case.

The unique features of ideological change in Tunisia under the Western impact can best be illustrated by comparison with a norm—with an ideal pattern of change from a static to a dynamic society in the colonial situation. This can be viewed as a four-stage process.

First, there is a period of quiescence and gestation following the establishment of Western control. If any modernizing movement existed before the Western domination, such a movement becomes for a time disorganized.

A second stage follows in which a small elite, usually more an informal cultural association than a political party, consciously imitates the colonizer. This elite tends to see its mission as twofold—to prove to the colonizer that the native population is "civilizable" and to serve as the vanguard in showing the native population the way to "salvation." But this elite faces an inherent dilemma: Its very reasonableness in this honeymoon period may win the prize of assimilation—but for the elite only, thus risking loss of identity with its own culture. If this danger is to be surmounted, the elite must attract popular support in the third stage.

Even if this transition is accomplished smoothly, it involves making compromises on the ideological plane, for the leadership must trim its sails to appeal to the more conservative masses. In the third stage, with the formation of a mass movement, moderation vis-à-vis the colonizer is no longer possible. The impulse toward political agitation, extremism, and demagogy is matched by a tendency to assert native individuality, by a studied rejection of any and all colonial innovations—a sort of return to the womb.

Out of this disequilibrium emerges a fourth, and usually final, stage of the colonial situation. This may take either of two forms. On the one hand, the major problems of old versus new, indigenous versus extraneous, and conservatism versus the idea of progress may be submerged in an all-out national struggle for independence. This might appear both logical and reasonable, but it actually means simply postponing consideration of problems that must eventually be faced. On the other hand, the difficult adjustment of new, alien ideas to the traditional, indigenous culture may be carried out at the same time as the struggle for national independence. This course may weaken the front against the colonizer and thus delay the attainment of independence, but it gains time for the alien ideas to be digested. The new state may thus come to independence with something approaching a new national ideology.

Ideally, each of the first three stages should come in order and be allowed to mature before being succeeded by the next stage. In the fourth stage, also, there should be a continuing process of assimilation and change rather than a simple postponement of the ideological conflict. The whole process of transition is in danger if there is too great a departure from this ideal pattern. Thus, the first stage is frustrated, as in Morocco and Algeria, if there are too many local uprisings and if public security is not quickly and efficiently secured.

It is even more important that the second stage, when the elite consciously imitates the colonizing culture, run its course before the attempt at national mass organization begins. The premature appearance of the Watani Party of Mustafa Kamil in Egypt in the early 1900's forced the moderates into the role of rather ineffective politicians before they could achieve an intellectual reconciliation between the alien and the indigenous cultures. This second stage was more nearly ideal in India, Sudan, Tunisia, and perhaps Lebanon and Syria, where it took place during a period of Western influence but before the establishment of overt Western control.

A major consideration in the third stage is that the Westernizing elite be fully committed to change and politically effective if it is to prevent the formation of a reactionary ("return to the precolonial golden age") movement.

In several countries, in the fourth stage, ideological debate was postponed in favor of total involvement in the struggle for national independence; among these were Egypt under the Wafd, Morocco under the Istiqlal, and Pakistan. The ideological debate continued during the national struggle for independence in Lebanon, Algeria, and Tunisia.

One might advance here the assertion that Tunisia has come as close as any colonized state to following the "ideal" path of development from static to dynamic society, which would explain its present acceptance of commitment to change. But before testing this assertion, it is important to mention two factors that remained constant in all four stages of Tunisia's development and largely determined the course of her development.

First, in considering the Western impact, one must realize that the receiving society was much more than just an inert force ready to be shaped by outside influences. When French occupation started in 1881, Tunisia had long been a unified country, possessing all the institutions of a viable society. It did not have to discover that it was a state; thus it could concentrate on the task of becoming a modern state.

Second, the presence of foreign settlers—which can be either an asset or an obstacle—proved in Tunisia an effective means of speeding up the process of social and ideological development. This did not happen by design. Rather, a happy combination of circumstances willed that the very factor at the root of the difficulties in Algeria served to accelerate the process of ideological modernization in Tunisia.

How closely Tunisia's experience followed the suggested ideal pattern of development will be seen in the following chapters on changes in Tunisia during the period of the French Protectorate.

2. The First Stage: Early Western Impact

In the early days of the Protectorate, Paul Lapie, a French professor in Tunis, in trying to define the "Arab mentality," made these observations:

> The Arab is a dreamer, but his reverie does not get lost in the future. It is made of memories more than hopes. Generous, charitable, and unselfish, the Arab owes all his traits to his improvidence. . . . Political economy is for the Moslem only the art of conserving natural riches. True wealth is not the work of man; it is a spontaneous product of nature. Man does not need to create, but only to maintain. Between the lane and the highway there is the same difference as between the beylical state and a European state. The fortuitous succession of men and horses traces the lane from day to day. On the contrary, to construct a highway, and above all a system of highways, a prior plan is needed. It is no longer chance circumstance but rather the farsighted will of men that decides. . . . The beylical state is not intended to foresee future injustices but only to put down past ones.[1]

Tunisia in 1881 had a population of about 1.3 million, only half of whom lived in settled communities. In addition to thousands of true nomads, there were many seminomads who farmed on a sharecropping basis until a rainless year or suddenly increased taxes made a return to nomadism more attractive. To the wary Tunisian bourgeois or small farmer along the intensively cultivated coast line, the beylical state governed best when it governed least. A good ruler was one who managed to keep the Bedouins under control without raising taxes.

What little public service existed was nongovernmental. It centered in the guilds of urban artisans or tradesmen, which were closely allied with the religious brotherhoods, and in the Islamic system of pious trusts (*habous,* or *waqfs*). Under this system, a donor could provide for a hospital or a primary school (*kuttab*), maintain a mosque or a brotherhood headquarters (*zawiya*), or ensure his family's future by placing his property under religious trust, thereby safeguarding it against government confiscation and allowing designated heirs to live off the revenue until the family line was extinct.

The "government" consisted of a small group around the ruling bey, mainly of Turkish origin (even those of other nationalities, such as the Circassian Kheireddine, thought of themselves as Turks), and tribal sheiks whose loyalty to the bey hinged upon his ability to enforce his will. Taxes were collected in tribal areas by military campaigns. With luck, a show of force sufficed and the taxes were forthcoming. Otherwise, the settled population might well find its own taxes increased to make up the deficit. Since there were only 2.5 miles of paved roads in the beylic, it was often more economical to let the remoter tribes have their own way so long as they did not seriously disturb the settled areas.

Everything in this system worked toward a cautious maintenance of the *status quo*. If a man got too rich in trade or in government, his property might be confiscated. If an enlightened governor wanted to improve public services, the populace, seeing only the prospect of increased taxes, would kill the projects by their passive resistance. The cultivated areas bordering the nomadic domain were subject to tribal raids. The land and property placed in pious trusts as a protective measure fell into disuse because it was in no one's interest to maintain them.

Yet hopelessly static as pre-Protectorate Tunisia might appear, there was much in Tunisian society that was sound and could serve as a foundation for development. Unlike many other states of Africa and Western Asia, Tunisia was blessed with a relatively homogeneous population with a long tradition of living together and of considering itself a single society. There was one national language. Arabic (only a few thousand Berber-speaking inhabitants remained at this time), and except for a fairly well integrated Jewish community, a single national religion, Islam. Furthermore, Tunisian Moslems, unlike those of Iraq or the Indian subcontinent, were not split into opposing sects; nearly all Tunisian Moslems belonged to the orthodox Sunni community.

Finally, although the settling of the nomad was a necessary prelude to any effective economic development, there was the unbroken tradition of settled life along Tunisia's long coast line, from Bizerte in the northwest around Cape Bon, and down the eastern coast as far south as Sfax. This region nurtured a people who were frugal and hard-working and held knowledge in great esteem. Particularly in the Sahel—Arabic for "coast"— which extended north and south from Sousse, with a village every three or four miles (in contrast to Morocco, where villages and towns were few), there was a thriving civilization dating from the time of the Carthaginian state. With a certain shared tradition and an orderly life based on a relatively high level of urbanization, the Sahel, the real Tunisia, was much further along the road to modernization than the European might have realized. Great changes could be made with the addition of only two major ingredients—greater public security and the concept of the positive state.

An Early Innovator

A dozen years before the establishment of the French Protectorate, a serious step toward modernizing Tunisia had been attempted by Kheireddine Pasha—later to be called "Abu al Nahda" ("Father of the Reawakening"). A Circassian Mameluke and member of the small Turkish ruling class, he was Premier of Tunisia from 1873 to 1877.

Kheireddine, author of a handbook of practical reforms for Moslem states, had much in common with such modernizing statesmen as Mohammed Ali of Egypt and Sultan Mahmud II and Midhat Pasha, both of the Ottoman Empire. These men argued as follows: Islam is valid, yet Moslems today are weak; Western civilization, although certainly less valid, appears stronger; to right the balance, Moslems must return to their true path, to the fundamentals of their religion, and must at the same time learn the technical skills that have given Western civilization its temporary superiority.

It is clear why both secularists and Islamic reformers could claim spiritual kinship with this school of thought. Yet later generations were to realize that the return to Islamic fundamentalism and the adoption of modern techniques cannot be carried out simultaneously. Each of these goals must be painfully reinterpreted; the bridging of the intellectual chasm between the two by some form of apologetics is a poor alternative.

The basic assumptions of Islamic culture were never questioned by Kheireddine and his followers. Impressed by the efficiency and strength of the West, they sought to integrate Western techniques into the indigenous culture. Education was to be their prime tool, and it is significant that the most important and lasting of Kheireddine's efforts was the founding, in 1875, of Sadiki College.* Staffed with foreign and native teachers, the college was to provide the cadres of the new Tunisia. Still, it was less a modern secular school than one patterned after those that had trained the leaders of the medieval Mameluke regime in Egypt. Western education came only after a thorough grounding in Arabic and Islamic studies. The decree establishing Sadiki College expresses this clearly. The school was

> . . . to teach the Koran, writing, and useful knowledge, i.e., juridical sciences, foreign languages, and the rational sciences that might be of use to Moslems, being at the same time not contrary to the faith. The professors must inculcate in the students love of the faith by showing them its beauties and excellence, in telling them the deeds of the Prophet, the miracles accomplished by Him, the virtues of holy men. . . .

By 1878, the school had a student body of 189. The students' first years were spent in Islamic studies, after which the curriculum consisted of modern subjects taught by foreigners in French, Italian, and Turkish. A French teacher in Algeria reported that, on the whole, the college was superior to comparable French

---

* Named after the reigning bey, Mohammed el Sadik, the college was financed by the funds confiscated from the preceding premier, Kheireddine's father-in-law.

schools in Algeria.[2] In a few years, however, most of the funds of the school were frittered away through mismanagement or siphoned off by corrupt administrators, and standards declined sharply.

A similar fate overtook Kheireddine's other reforms—his attempts to modernize the army and to institute tax and land reforms. He was dismissed from his post as Pasha because of a combination of internal and external pressures, and left for Constantinople, where he later became Grand Vizier. Ironically, the man who had tried to modernize the Tunisian state in time to avoid Western interference paved the way, through the sale of his large land holdings to a French joint stock company, for the real beginning of French colonization four years before the establishment of the Protectorate. His act neatly symbolizes the close of one era and the opening of another.

But much endured of the first Tunisian modernist movement. Sadiki College and the tutelage of the great Pasha largely formed the next generation of national leaders. Even more important, future reformers could refute accusations that they advocated foreign ideas by claiming to be the spiritual heirs of the Father of the Reawakening.

The Protectorate

In 1881, after a brief military campaign, a reluctant bey was forced to accept the French Protectorate. The native leadership was either in rout or cautiously studying how to come to grips with this new situation. For the next few years, the most important stimulus for change came from the European settlers. Instead of being an experience limited to a small elite, the contact with modernism became a face-to-face encounter on all levels of Tunisian society.

The French Protectorate, which lasted seventy-five years, had immeasurable ramifications on the development of Tunisia. Independent Tunisia inherited from the Protectorate the rudiments of a modern economy, and this material foundation played a vital role in conditioning the Tunisian mentality to modernism.

For the moment, however, let us merely keep the economic aspect of development in mind as a constant factor, while trying to isolate the major variables that played a part in reshaping the Tunisian mentality.

With the French Protectorate came a greater measure of public security. The Bedouins were largely brought under control, and within a few years the area of sedentary cultivation began encroaching on their boundaryless domain. The regular, orderly collection of taxes was equally novel, although taxes continued to weigh heavily on the small cultivator.

The French Administration in Tunisia was inclined to be conservative, carefully maintaining the beylical state and the various religious institutions. The official French colonial policy that "It is necessary to have them evolve within the framework of their own civilization,"[3] was welcomed by such early officials as Bernard Roy, long-time Secretary General, and Louis Machuel, first Director of Education. These men were noted Arabists, so absorbed in Moslem mores that they could often be seen strolling the streets carrying a *subha*, the Moslem rosary. Another high French official, D'Estournelles de Constant, wrote an influential book insisting that the Tunisian state be changed as little as possible and urging that European colonization be discouraged: "Let us not seek to make pseudo-Europeans of the [the Tunisians]. Let us remember that fifty years of living with us have passed over the Algerians without modifying them."[4]

This attempt to shield Tunisia from the ruder shocks of Western penetration was nevertheless doomed by the steady flow of European settlers.* By the 1890's, the French administrators, fearing the unmistakable Italian designs on Tunisia, inaugurated an official program of colonization in order to

* In the first ten years of the Protectorate, the French population jumped from 3,393 to more than 10,000. In 1895, the total European population was estimated at more than 77,000—20,000 French and French protégés, 40,000 Italians, and 15,000 Maltese constituted the major groups. Numerically, the Italian settlers exceeded the French until as late as 1931. Yet their influence in Tunisia was so much less than that of the French—who were, of course, both settlers and administrators—that they receive little attention in the following pages.

settle more French citizens in the Protectorate. With this growing French and European community came demands for schools,
roads, a French legal system, legislation to facilitate exploitation
of land and resources—in short, a whole roster of claims designed to provide a modern, Western existence for the Europeans of Tunisia.

In contrast to Algeria, colonized fifty years earlier, where the
effects of Western penetration never filtered down to the native
masses, Tunisia benefited from a happy synthesis of conflicting
elements. The aggressive capitalistic initiative of the French
settler (*colon*), the feeling of "stewardship" toward the local
population manifested by the leading Protectorate officials, the
native Tunisian attitude of eclectic acceptance—all joined to push
Tunisia into the modern world without destroying the foundations of Tunisian society.

Although the two worlds confronted each other in all spheres
of activity, in the towns and in the countryside, it was in education and agriculture that the impact of the Europeans was
greatest and that there was the most widespread intermingling of
the two communities. Therefore, the reforms in these two fields
may best illustrate the effect of Western colonization on the
Tunisian way of life.

Tunisia already had its own educational system. Higher
education was centered in Zitouna University, with nearly 1,000
students; below this was a network of about 1,400 Islamic primary
schools, or *kuttabs,* with an attendance of almost 20,000. The
enrollment was more impressive than the results, however. In
the *kuttab,* a scarcely literate teacher drilled his little circle of
students, aged five to sixteen, in memorizing the Koran. Graduates often could not read the simplest secular texts and seldom
could write. Even at Zitouna University, only about 100 students
pursued what might properly be called higher education. For
most, their education fitted them only for the profession of Islamic
teacher or cadi (judge) in Sharia (Islamic religious law) courts.
Only Sadiki College educated Tunisians for the modern world.
As for the pre-Protectorate private European schools, most of
which were Catholic, in 1880 they had only 4 Tunisian Moslems

among their students. The Protectorate policy was to leave the *kuttabs* and Zitouna University alone; they were deemed private schools and were subjected to a minimum of inspection and state regulation.

The clamor of the European community brought about a new national school system, completely French except for minor changes to fit the situation in Tunisia. All instruction was in French, with Arabic and Italian as second languages; the history and geography of North Africa were also included in the curriculum. In theory, these schools, supported by the Tunisian budget, were free and open to all races and religions, but in fact, it was often easy to turn away the Tunisian Moslem because he was not sufficiently prepared, did not know French well enough, or was too old. Nor were tradition-bound parents more willing than elsewhere in the Arab world to send their children to European schools. The principle of universal public education was nevertheless established, and in time, the results were significant.*

In the early years, there was considerable intermixture of Europeans and Tunisians in the classes. In 1899, all but nineteen of the seventy-eight boys' or joint boys' and girls' public schools had Moslems and Europeans studying side by side. Something approaching segregation began with the inauguration of the Franco-Arab schools designed especially for Tunisian Moslems. These schools evolved both from the natural desire of the local population to maintain some instruction in their own language and from the growing prejudices of *colons* against having Tunisians studying with their children. In principle, however, the completely French schools remained open to qualified Moslems. The Franco-Arab system was basically French

* Although in 1899 the one French *lycée*, or secondary school, had only 10 Tunisian Moslems compared with 160 Tunisian Jews and 338 French, the situation in the primary grades was much more encouraging. The table shows the total primary-school attendance in the public schools for the same year.

	French	Italians	Tunisian Moslems	Jews	Others	Totals
BOYS	1,532	1,801	3,782	1,193	822	9,130
GIRLS	1,017	1,466	31	1,101	658	4,273

in its outlines, with some emphasis on Arabic and Islamic studies; only about one-third of the instruction was in Arabic. The standards of these schools approached those of the completely French schools.

Sadiki College had its ups and downs in the early years of the Protectorate, but by the mid-1890's, it was recognized as the archetype for the secondary level of the growing Franco-Arab system. It had returned once again to fulfilling the function intended by Kheireddine Pasha—that of preparing cadres for running a modern state.

The very Europeans whose presence had the unintended result of giving Tunisia the basis of a sound, modern educational system were at the same time giving her a severe jolt on the agricultural front. Coming to a country where land was an inheritance and agriculture an unchanging way of life, the French capitalists and *colons* introduced, in addition to modern mechanized farming, the novel idea of land as a commodity and agriculture as a capitalistic venture.

Before the Protectorate, the total amount of land under cultivation was as low as 1.5 million acres. Absence of public order, arbitrary and fluctuating taxes, and an ill-defined, regressive system of land ownership were the major reasons for the high proportion of idle acreage. We have seen that the establishment of the Protectorate eliminated the first two problems; let us now see how it affected the third.

The question of land ownership in pre-Protectorate Tunisia was often far from clear. Much of the land was state domain obtained by confiscation. Another large share, perhaps as much as 40 per cent of the arable land, was given over to *habous*. Each *habous*, inalienable in principle, was managed by an administrator who received only token payment for his services and had no incentive to improve the land. The beneficiaries seldom pressed for more profitable use, since their number was usually so great that no single one could hope to benefit significantly from any improvement. As a result, *habous* lands were easily recognized by their run-down appearance.

There was also an indeterminate amount of land held as private property (*mulk*), but boundaries were poorly defined and deeds were unregistered. Ownership rights were generally based on custom—a combination of prescriptive right and village acceptance. In addition, the Islamic law of inheritance, which rejects primogeniture in favor of division among a number of specified heirs, soon cut any piece of land into many segments, unless the original owner had managed to circumvent the law of inheritance by setting up a private *habous*. Nor was it uncommon for a wary owner of property in *mulk* to have hidden in reserve a *habous* title to the same property—as a protection against the danger of government confiscation.

Finally, there were the great areas of the Bedouins' pastoral lands. Parts of this land might be claimed by the state, by *habous*, or even by private individuals, but the dominant fact was the existence of the tribe on the spot, convinced of its rights of usage.

Within a decade after the Treaty of Bardo, establishing the Protectorate, French holdings in Tunisia amounted to just over 1 million acres. This period of rampant speculation and large capitalistic holdings was followed by one of intensive colonization. In 1897, a colonization fund to purchase land for French settlement was set up, and the next year, an Ecole Coloniale d'Agriculture was founded to train *colons* for settlement in Tunisia.

The old balance was irretrievably shattered. Land that had been surrendered to nomadism since the eleventh century was now returned to cultivation, and the Bedouins were forced to settle down or withdraw.* In addition, the sharecropper,

---

* The most striking example was in the governorate of Sfax, where an enterprising Director of Agriculture became convinced that this region, cultivated in Roman and Byzantine days, could again produce olives. Since the olive tree requires twelve to fifteen years before giving a good yield, this was a long-term investment. French capital provided the needed funds; Tunisians from the area worked the land under a contract (*mugharasa*) that gave them full property rights to 50 per cent of the land when developed. As a result, Sfax, which had only 45,000 acres of olive trees in 1881, had more than 500,000 acres in cultivation by 1907.

or *khammas*,* was jolted out of his old routine. Under the new European owner, he became an agricultural laborer, probably earning much more than before but exposed to the unaccustomed rigors of a dynamic, capitalist timetable. Much like the English peasant in the early decades of the Industrial Revolution, the Tunisian farmer was pushed from a world of status to one of contract, and whether he was better off or more miserable depends on whether one agrees, for instance, with David Ricardo or with William Cobbett. For better or worse, the revolution was on, and the Tunisian farmer was learning modern techniques, French customs, and the French language.

As land gained in value, the loose system of landholding became intolerable. In 1885, the Land Registration Act was passed. Under the provisions of this act, a man could present a property claim that would be registered if not challenged after due publicity and specified period of time; a title deed would then be issued by a special Tribunal Mixte, composed of French and Tunisian magistrates. Registration was not mandatory, because property law was very much tied in with Islamic Sharia law, and compliance with the act meant taking a broad step away from traditional Islamic law. Yet a surprising number of Tunisians, as well as all Europeans seeking land, took advantage of this act.† Even *habous* lands were offered for registration, as the Tribunal Mixte had decided it had jurisdiction in this area also.

Not only did every Tunisian petitioner for land receive a firsthand lesson in the workings of Western law, but he also remained thereafter intimately linked with that system and interested in understanding it. Since all litigation involving registered property went before the French courts in Tunisia, the Tunisian had implicitly removed himself from Sharia jurisdiction in this important field. Land registration, therefore,

---

* A derivative of the Arabic word for "five"; in theory, the *khammas* received one-fifth of the yield of the land he worked.

† By 1907, the Tribunal Mixte had received requests for registration from 3,331 French settlers, 2,824 non-French settlers, and 3,985 Tunisians. By 1936, the figures were 6,363 French, 5,000 non-French, and 11,230 Tunisians. At the time of independence, just under 5 million acres had been registered.

spread Western ideas and downgraded the traditional courts —all without a direct attack on the Islamic legal system.

In sharp contrast to the major roles played by education and land reform in the process of modernization is the relatively minor part played by the introduction of modern democratic government. Even the presence of a large French community demanding the "rights of Frenchmen" was not enough to force the creation of representative institutions in Tunisia. Tunis had possessed a municipal council since 1858. After the Protectorate was established, other municipalities were granted councils, which remained, however, under central control and were assured French majorities. The same conservatism existed in national representation. A Consultative Conference was established, and in 1905, the French community gained the right to elect delegates to its three "colleges"—agricultural, commercial, and a third that represented all other French interests, mainly the civil service. Two years later, native representatives were added, but they were appointed by the Protectorate Government. The Consultative Conference was to remain only an advisory body, with very limited powers.

The French penchant for highly centralized, direct administration held sway. The Protectorate Government relied on the old ruling families, the provincial governors (*caïds*), and religious leaders (ulema) to make its rule more palatable to the populace, finding support in the argument that since France was required by the Treaty of Bardo to protect the autocratic bey, French authorities could scarcely foster representative institutions or decentralization, which would reduce the beylical "sovereign" power.

Does the case of Tunisia, where rapid adjustment to modernization took place in the almost complete absence of grass-roots democracy, suggest that representative government is best postponed until after the colonial experience, or even, perhaps, that representative government introduced before a certain stage in the change from static to dynamic society makes the transition more difficult? One hesitates to advance a general rule, but it seems to have been true among the Tunisian elite that since they had virtually no representation, their attention was directed toward other problems. Perhaps the absence of any such "distraction" left the Tunisians free to work out the imposing problem of adapting their traditional society to the exigencies of the modern world.

What, then, were the activities of the native elite during the first years of the Protectorate? In the first stage, one would expect the elite to be quiescent, attempting to understand the new conditions. This was the case in Tunisia. The disciples of Kheireddine dropped temporarily into the background. Several of them went into exile, but most took a wait-and-see attitude. This reaction of moderation and good sense closely paralleled that of the great Egyptian Moslem reformer, Sheik Mohammed Abduh, who had visited Tunisia in 1884. Considering outright resistance to Western domination useless, they concentrated on schemes of reform from within, while making the best of Western occupation and even, on occasion, taking advantage of it.[5]

Tunisian leaders, for example, were able to convince the French to recruit Sadiki College graduates for the administration as translators and minor officials, posts formerly held by Lebanese and Syrians. Soon about thirty young men representing that element of the elite most disposed by past training to understand and absorb Western culture were integrated into the administration, and especially into the Direction de l'Enseignement. This was a small step, but one of great symbolic importance: The Tunisian elite, the heirs of Kheireddine, were willing to accept French tutelage in order to advance their aims of modernization.

Al Hadira, the first unofficial Arabic-language newspaper in Tunisia, was founded in 1888 in this same spirit.[6] The paper was edited by a Sadiki College graduate, and the contributors included nearly all the former followers of Kheireddine, the most influential being Bechir Sfar, who was eventually to earn the sobriquet "Second Father of the Reawakening." *Al Hadira* was apolitical, seeing its task as that of educating the people in modernization. For example, the very circumspect articles about *bid'a* (blameworthy innovation) in Islam were designed to lessen the power of the religious brotherhoods, always a potential influence against change. The articles stressing the need for education of women—it was too soon even to suggest removing the veil—found in the early issues of *Al Hadira* might be deemed the first steps toward female emancipation in Tunisia.

Al Hadira's modernization and its refusal to engage in criticism of the Protectorate made it suspect in some circles; other newspapers that were suspended by the authorities probably reflected public opinion more faithfully. But *Al Hadira* represented an ideal—modernization—while other papers tended to lapse into an unimaginative standpattism. As a result of *Al Hadira*'s influence, even the most conservative newspapers soon felt obliged to evoke the memory of Kheireddine and to talk of *islah* (reform).

It was chiefly the *Al Hadira* group who, in 1896, founded the Khaldouniya (named for Ibn Khaldoun, the famous Arab historian, born in Tunis in 1332), an institution designed to offer modern studies to Zitouna University students, who were still completely submerged in a curriculum of medieval religious formalism. The founders worked closely with French authorities, and the school was begun with the active support of French Resident General René Millet. The Khaldouniya was an important landmark; it was not only an attempt to recruit the Zitouna youth to the idea of modernization, but also the first organized attempt by private Tunisian citizens to achieve civic improvement. It was, in the Western sense, the first Tunisian "society" and it provided "the country's first experience with a system of elections, conferences, and peaceful debate on public affairs."[7]

With the establishment of the Khaldouniya, many of those who had been trained at Sadiki College and in France tried, for the first time, to explain in Arabic their new ideas to compatriots still entrenched in the traditional culture. As with Sadiki College, one cannot measure the importance of the Khaldouniya in numbers. The first year, there was an average of only seventy-one students attending the courses at any one time, and as late as 1905, the number had barely doubled.[8] As was to be expected, the Khaldouniya faced the scarcely concealed opposition of most of the Zitouna ulema: Although religious prophets are often revolutionary, religious hierarchies can almost never be other than conservative. However, it may have been fortunate that the Khaldouniya and its related activities had only a limited success, for this prevented a premature step to the stage of mass movements.

The Khaldouniya marks the turning point from the first to the second stage of Tunisian development under the colonial influence—the move from passivity to a more dynamic self-assertion, to a period in which an attempt is made to formulate a new indigenous ideology.

3. Stage Two: The Young Tunisians, or, The Age of Reason

It would be the rare Western observer who would not be impressed by, and in sympathy with, the small group who made up the "Young Tunisian" movement at the turn of the century. Cultured, well-educated, and of a rigorous intellectual honesty, they tackled with vigor the task of mediating between the dominant alien culture and their own society.

Since it is tempting to contrast the virtues of the Young Tunisians with the failings of the Old Destour Party of the next generation, it is only fair to preface an analysis of their role with an explanatory reservation. Most of the Young Tunisians came from the close-knit Tunisian aristocracy, largely Turkish in origin. They were accustomed to the idea of leading, and had been trained for this task. Most of them were graduates of Sadiki College, and many had also studied in France. Since direct national leadership was barred by the presence of the French, it was natural that they should move into the role of spokesmen to the French for the *indigène* and interpreters of things French to their own people.

They were fortunate not only to be psychologically and intellectually fitted for their chosen role, but also to be living in a period when the traditional, hierarchical society was still largely intact. Had it been their fate to attempt the next generation's task of organizing a mass movement, with the old society crumbling and the new far from ready to take its place, their record might not have been so good. The Young Tunisians—the Fabian Society of the Tunisian national movement—had a more consistent ideology than the Old Destour. But each movement must be judged on the basis of the part it had to play.

22

The name "Young Tunisian"* is, of course, copied from the Young Turk movement, and like the Young Turks, the Young Tunisians attempted to modernize and Westernize a traditional Islamic society. The organization was more a coterie of like-minded young men than a political party. Although they claimed a membership of 1,000–1,500, this figure included both participants and sympathizers. Most of the activities and writings of the Young Tunisians can be traced to about a dozen persons.

The founding of the Khaldouniya, in 1896, might be called the beginning of the movement, for it was an attempt by the "modern" elite to capture for reformism the major bastions of reaction, the ulema and Zitouna University. The Khaldouniya was concerned primarily with explaining Western ideas to Tunisians. The Young Tunisian movement was equally concerned with the task of explaining itself to the French rulers. In 1906, two Tunisians were invited to participate in the French Colonial Congress at Marseilles, and for the first time the ideas of the Young Tunisians were brought to the attention of the French liberals. Their reports, especially those of Mohammed Lasram, Director of the Khaldouniya, sketched a sound and moderate program of proposed reforms.† The predominant theme was a call for Franco-Tunisian cooperation to achieve a modern liberal state. Lasram's report on "Means to Accelerate the Rapprochement of the Two Races" concluded by recommending more instruction in both the Arabic and French languages, and more social contact between the French and Tunisian communities. Lasram added that French colonization was acceptable, provided it went hand in hand with what he termed "indigenous colonization"—that is, the native population should have equal chances at land and at modern methods of farming in order to learn from the example of the French *colon*.

Many elements of the French Radical Socialist and Socialist

* The term was employed in Tunisia as early as 1898. (Cf. Paul Lapie, *Les Civilisations Tunisiennes* [Paris, 1898], p. 182.)

† Lasram's reports, which covered a wide field, including the Khaldouniya, the private *habous*, indigenous provident societies, primary and secondary education, and the religious brotherhoods, bear the mark of thoughtful research and scholarship that make them useful historical sources to this day.

parties began to support what they saw as the basically as-
similationist position of the Young Tunisians, and the Young
Tunisians became even more impressed with the concept of
the "other France"—the France of liberal democracy, the rights
of man, and a universal society transcending race or religion.
They hoped that the support of this France would aid in the
evolution of Tunisian society and more than offset the arrogance and presumptuous claims of the *colon* party in Tunisia.*

This was the background for the establishment, in February,
1907, of *Le Tunisien,* the first French-language newspaper edited
by Tunisians. The founders of *Le Tunisien* were fighting for
the support of French public opinion, both in Tunisia and in
France, and at the same time working out among themselves
a program of reform and action. Their view of their own countrymen was outspokenly elitist. They saw their task as one of
arousing other Tunisians from their "intellectual torpor."[1]

The paper appeared weekly for just over five years (until
March, 1912). There were only a half-dozen regular contributors,
and of these, Ali Bach Hamba and Abdel Djelil Zaouche were
by far the most important. It would be incorrect to term these
two men typical of the Young Tunisians, for both were activists
of the Teddy Roosevelt variety—a rare phenomenon in the
Tunisia of the time.

Bach Hamba, a Tunisian aristocrat of Turkish origin, studied
a few years at Zitouna Mosque, but it was Sadiki College that
largely shaped his ideas. After graduating from Sadiki, he stayed
on as an administrative officer while preparing himself for his
French law degree. As editor of *Le Tunisien* and a driving force
behind the myriad activities of the Association des Anciens
Elèves de Sadiki (founded in 1905), Bach Hamba most nearly
deserves the title of leader of the Young Tunisians. He was a
theorist, but one who pursued his ideals with all the persistence
and courage of a Turkish soldier. He was, one suspects, often
somewhat pleased with the daring of his stand. When *Le*

---

* The term *"colon* party" is used here to represent the views of the majority of French settlers, and does not mean a political organization, although
the *colons* were at various times organized into political groups.

Tunisien was closed in 1912, Bach Hamba's pride dictated a clean break with Tunisia. He went into exile and died in Constantinople in 1918, on the day the Allied armies entered the city.

Zaouche, an aristocrat like Bach Hamba, had a thoroughly French education at the Lycée St. Charles (now the Lycée Carnot) in Tunis and the Faculté de Droit in Paris. He spoke and read classical Arabic with difficulty, and a Tunisian who knew Zaouche observed that he would have had difficulty in explaining the difference between a mosque and a *zawiya*. A man of great energy, a pragmatist, and a diplomat, he was a successful businessman, the leading Tunisian member of the Consultative Conference, a major contributor to *Le Tunisien*, active in other clubs and organizations, and particularly resourceful in the formulation and implementation of practical self-help schemes.

A third man should be introduced here as an example of the sort of person the Young Tunisians were influencing: Sheik Abdelaziz Taalbi, who was to lead the Old Destour Party after World War I. Although identified with the Young Tunisian movement as editor of the Arabic edition of *Le Tunisien*, he was in basic disagreement with its thinking, and his alliance, however sincere, was bound to break in time. His views were formed at the Khaldouniya, where he was greatly influenced by Bechir Sfar. Taalbi approached modernism not as an end in itself, to be reconciled to Islam only insofar as possible, but rather as a tool to be used in making Islam stronger and more in tune with the times. Taalbi's approach was closer to that of the Islamic reform group in Egypt which, starting as a liberal and even bold departure, ended as an intellectual movement in apologetics and a mass movement in the Moslem Brotherhood.

Early in Taalbi's career, some Moslem savants brought heresy charges against him, but at his death, he was identified with these same "old turbans." It was not Taalbi but Tunisia that had changed.

The Young Tunisians, on the other hand, espoused a cause which, though not necessarily anticlerical or irreligious, logically ended in a form of secularism with a clear-cut distinction between the religious institution and the state.

Le Tunisien remains as a monument to this first Tunisian modernist movement and to the honeymoon period in the relations between protector and protégé. The ideology of the group evolved around four major themes: (1) the formation of a new brand of Tunisian patriotism within the colonial framework; (2) the concept of the positive state; (3) the role of education; and (4) the development of a critical faculty accompanied by an absence of apologetics.

The Young Tunisian Brand of Patriotism

The Young Tunisians claimed to be patriots who were not hostile to France. As the French-educated Tunisian elite, they wanted to transmit what they had learned from France to the rest of their countrymen. "Our new mentality is formed by French civilization. We have appropriated its vast domain. We have made it ours," stated an editorial in *Le Tunisien*.[2] This meant an open acceptance of a *politique de rapprochement et d'association;* there was no thought of independence. In fact, an article written as late as 1910 viewed naturalization as the best solution for French North Africa—then Algeria and Tunisia—provided the Moslem was permitted to keep his Moslem personal status (i.e., be subject to the Sharia court in such matters as marriage and inheritance).[3] Basically, the Young Tunisians were asking for equality, for the "rights of Frenchmen"; that this might mean some kind of permanent political relationship with France was no cause for alarm. Thus, Zaouche voiced the hope that once Tunisians exhibited a "French mentality" as proof of loyalty, they would be treated no differently "from Normans, Bretons, or Corsicans."[4]

To the Young Tunisians, the real community was the *patrie* rather than the traditional Islamic *millet,* or religious community. At a time when the Tunisian Jewish leaders were pressing for access to French courts, with the ultimate aim of French citizenship, the Young Tunisians insisted that the Jews remain

Tunisian citizens.* "Let us talk as Tunisians and not as Moslems or Jews," wrote Bach Hamba. "The time of confessional distinctions is past. It is the task of the young generations to work that they be completely forgotten."[5]

In wanting the "rights of Frenchmen" and in choosing the modern secular state instead of the *millet,* the Young Tunisians were placing their program and ideology on a plane where the question of religion was irrelevant. It was not that they rejected Islam; rather, it was to them merely a part of the cultural heritage of the Tunisian nation. The essence of their argument to the French was: Judge us by your own standards. This accepted, we will together—Young Tunisian and French—work to see that the rest of our Tunisian compatriots have a chance to achieve the same goal.

The extremist *colon* press always responded that the Tunisian Moslem, qua Moslem, could never become modern in the Western sense, and at the same time fanned the fires of anti-Semitism by declaring that the Jews were the only assimilable Tunisians. They claimed that when the chips were down, the Tunisians, like all other Moslems, would display religious fanaticism. In 1910, the extremists took advantage of the new Ottoman political orientation toward Germany to insist that the Young Tunisians were pro-Turk, pan-Islamic, and thus by definition anti-French. Bach Hamba was provoked into answering: "If modern educa-

---

* When a large Moslem meeting was organized to protest the December, 1909, vote of the Consultative Conference recommending that Jews have access to French courts, Ali Bach Hamba and other Young Tunisians refused to participate unless the meeting abandoned its anti-Jewish program, and unless the question of Jews having access to French courts was linked to the larger question of reforming the native courts.

The situation of the Tunisian and, more generally, the North African Jews is an interesting aspect of modern Jewish history which can only be briefly noted here. Generally speaking, Tunisian Jews assimilated the French language and culture much more quickly than their Moslem fellow countrymen (cf. the early education statistics mentioned above). Noting the example of Algerian Jews, who had been granted French citizenship en bloc in 1870, they favored separation from beylical authority and complete integration into the French community. This disparity of aims between the Moslem nationalists and the Jewish community could have deepened the anti-Jewish bias which was not lacking in Tunisia. It is to the credit of the Tunisian nationalists that such an eventuality was actively combated.

tion has given us a new mentality, we preserve nevertheless our individuality. As Moslems, we have a lively sympathy for our brothers in all countries. Turks and Egyptians inspire in us the same sentiment as our neighbors of Algeria or as the distant populations of Asia. There is nothing in this to call into question our loyalty to France, each country having its own destiny and its own aspirations."[6]

The Idea of the Positive State

For centuries, Tunisians had looked upon government as something best avoided, since its only apparent function was to collect taxes for its own maintenance. But just as the Tunisian fellah suddenly learned from his *colon* neighbor the possibilities of modern farming, so now the Young Tunisians saw that a modern state could carry out a social revolution. Their concept of the modern state was divided into two major aspects: what the state should be, and what the state should do.

The new state was to be a government of laws, not men. Western-style legal codes and a modern administrative system would make it possible for the citizen to know exactly what the law was on any subject at any time.* The Young Tunisians opposed the arbitrary state not so much because it was tyrannical, but because it was inefficient. Although some Frenchmen thought there was much that was good in the old system, to the Young Tunisians it spelled bribery, court favoritism, and arbitrary personal rule, all of which vitiated any chance of progress; for this reason it had to be replaced.

The Young Tunisians were neither democratic nor the contrary. They would have willingly adopted whichever route seemed best suited to bring about the modernization of Tunisia. They pushed for the popular election of the Tunisian section of the

---

* This is seen clearly in a number of articles on judicial reform by "Nassah'" (Hasan Guellaty), published in 1907 and 1908, calling for the separation of judicial and administrative powers, complete codes covering all justiciable matters, competent and well-paid personnel, a system of multiple recourse, and creation of courts that would permit collaboration between French and native magistrates.

Consultative Conference mainly for two reasons: First, the French and Tunisian communities should always be treated as equals, and, second, elections were unlikely to seat a more conservative group than those selected by the Protectorate Government. In 1910, Zaouche was able to get only four of his sixteen Tunisian colleagues in the Consultative Conference to sign a petition that they be elected rather than appointed in the coming session. As Bach Hamba noted in a bitter editorial, "The others thought—some even said out loud—that God would surely do whatever He wanted to do, and His creatures had only to follow their destiny. *Mektoub!* [It is written!]"[7] The Young Tunisians fully acknowledged that most of the Tunisian population was as yet reluctant to accept their program *in toto*. Their aim was a government for the people that would eventually make possible government of and by the people.

For that reason, they believed government should be strong. The classical concept of *laissez faire* was not subscribed to by the progressive elements in Tunisian society, or in any Moslem society, of the nineteenth or early twentieth centuries. The stimulus to change came from those whose backgrounds and traditions were in government and bureaucracy. Tunisia and other Moslem societies lacked the entrepreneurial class found in most Western states. The Young Tunisian knew that the Moslem merchant's outlook was static, that the craftsman's techniques were outmoded, and that the fellah's ignorance and poverty bound him to traditional ways. And one of the most disliked words in the vocabulary of the religious hierarchy was *bid'a* (innovation). It is small wonder the Young Tunisians held that the state must take action, else there would be no fruitful action at all.

Yet this group undertook the first genuine, privately organized projects of self-help in Tunisia—the Khaldouniya, modern Koranic schools, the public educational lectures given by the members of the Anciens de Sadiki, and the short-lived agricultural school for *indigènes*, patterned on the official French agricultural school for prospective settlers, to name only the most important. However, each of these organizations solicited government support, and most of them were started with a government subsidy. To the Young Tunisians, such private initiative was not so much an end in itself as a means to stimulate government action.

They were equally positive about what the ideal state should do. There were to be no sacrosanct areas in which the state could not intervene, with the single exception of the press. The Young Tunisians favored some government control over religion: They welcomed the governmental commission established to consider reform of the curriculum at Zitouna University; they urged the government "with the support of indigenous authorities" to suppress the deviations of *marabouts* (leaders of religious brotherhoods) and to control their propaganda.[8] They would give the state major, if not exclusive, responsibility in the field of education. They accepted the concept of official European colonization, provided the Protectorate Government took positive steps to place natives on the soil and train them in modern agricultural methods —a program they called "indigenous colonization." They could have advanced a strong argument against European colonization, but they chose rather to accept it if the Protectorate Government would exert identical efforts for the native population. This is an indication of the intensity of the Young Tunisians' commitment to positive government.

In sum, in their philosophy of the state, the Young Tunisians would have felt much more at home in Bourguiba's Tunisia than would many of the Old Destourians of the post-World War I period. Kheireddine Pasha would have felt at home, too, for that matter.

Education and French Culture

Education was the key concern of *Le Tunisien*. Perhaps as much as 25 per cent of the total coverage of the paper was devoted to this subject. This is not surprising, because there has seldom been a nationalist movement in a colonized country that has not loudly demanded more and better education. What distinguishes the Young Tunisians is the clarity with which they spelled out the type of modern education they wanted.

Most of them were familiar with the high quality of French education, and they were not willing to settle for anything inferior. Education in Tunisia should be in French; their slogan was: "Instruct in French and teach the Arab language."[9] Bach Hamba, trying to cover his flank from local attack, insisted that this aim was consistent with the program of Kheireddine Pasha, and that Sadiki College, founded *before* the Protectorate, was really the prototype of the Franco-Arab school. Two major justifications for education in French were pushed by the Young Tunisians: Tunisian youth needed an education in French in order to have an equal chance in the economic battle, and French (or at least some major European language) was the key to modernization. Only by knowing French could the fellah learn modern farming methods, the craftsman the use of machinery, the would-be trader the language and techniques of modern international trade, the civil servant the mechanics of a modern state.

Conservatives argued that modern ideas could be taught equally well in Arabic. Bach Hamba, with a rashness unmatched in the Arab world, emphatically denied this. Arabic, he affirmed, was "still far from adapting itself to scientific ideas." Although some people were captivated by the idea of Egypt, "The half century of Egyptian effort has not yet brought forth an original work. They have translated a great deal, imitated a great deal, but created almost nothing. And whatever is heard to the contrary, the Egyptian people remain on the margin of the scientific world." Then, giving the knife a final twist, Bach Hamba observed that the Egyptian works so often cited were, in fact, by authors who had received an education in a Western language, usually French.[10]

The hypersensitivity of the Young Tunisians on the question of education stemmed from their awareness of a real danger. The *colon* party and the Tunisian conservatives both had their own reasons for wanting to maintain the traditional Arabic-Islamic education in the *kuttab* and in Zitouna University. The French Rightists in Tunisia wanted, to paraphrase a term often used by the British in Egypt at this period, "Tunisian hands and French heads." The Tunisian conservatives, wanting to hold onto as much as possible of their own society, regarded the French Protectorate just as medieval Islamic society had regarded all government—as something to be neither loved nor hated, but merely respected for its force, and avoided as much as possible.

The Young Tunisians saw clearly that this was no way to build a modern nation-state. There must be a uniform school system for all Tunisia based on the French system. Schools could be thoroughly French—provided they were open to all on an equal basis. Or they could be Franco-Arab schools, teaching Arabic-Islamic studies and the history and geography of North Africa—provided they included *"the strict application of the program of French lay primary schools in its entirety."*[11] The Young Tunisians were skeptical of the practical trade schools. They feared that such schools would serve as a substitute for regular primary schools and thus bar the way to secondary and higher education for Tunisian Moslems.*

There were, however, differences among the Young Tunisians as to the best system of education. In 1906, Khairallah ben Mustafa, a Young Tunisian, set up in Tunis what he called a modern Koranic school, or "reformed *kuttab.*" Khairallah, who had studied at Sadiki and Alaoui colleges, was eager to use modern pedagogical techniques for teaching Arabic, and had written a book to express his views. He believed that Arabic, if properly taught, could serve as the base of a modern curriculum, and he worked to interest French officials in his plan. They urged him to solicit the support of Bechir Sfar, who, as President of the Habous Council, might be able to support such a model school with *habous* funds. Sfar eventually agreed, and the school was opened in December, 1906, in the old *medina* (Arab quarter) of Tunis.[12]

---

* This suspicion of practical trade schools or of any form of simplified education lasted throughout the Protectorate. In 1936, a French plan to eliminate illiteracy and give the rural population a basic education in agriculture by means of a three-year elementary course, taught by native monitors under direction of French teachers, came to grief through local opposition. The major argument was that this inferior education was useless for forming the needed cadres and that its existence would be used to justify delays in extending education of high standards.

The 1908 Congress on North Africa, held in Paris,* was also won over to Khairallah's position after hearing his well-documented report. Khairallah—like Bechir Sfar—was concerned with the necessity and desirability of maintaining much of the old. In his report to the Congress, he quoted the famous maxim of Le Bon, "*Respecter les traditions est une condition d'existence pour un peuple; savoir s'en dégager lentement, une condition de progrès.*" In Khairallah's view, the modern Koranic schools would serve as a sort of transitional system until such time as the network of Franco-Arab schools completely covered Tunisia. Although he had first planned to have all instruction in Arabic, he was later to become convinced of the need to give his students a good working knowledge of French. He did not break completely with the old system of memorizing the Koran by rote but recommended that those students not planning to specialize in religious studies later at Zitouna University be required to memorize only the first fifteen sections, roughly one-fourth of the whole.

But Bach Hamba, Zaouche, and many of the more radical Young Tunisians continued to oppose the modern Koranic schools for the same reason that they feared practical trade schools or segregated education. They felt it necessary to avoid at all costs a double standard in Tunisian education, for this would justify the French argument that top positions could be filled only by Frenchmen because of their better educational backgrounds. They also knew, although they were circumspect in saying so, that any attempt to combine the best elements of the two systems of education—traditional Islamic and modern French —would, given the conservatism of Tunisian public opinion, almost necessarily err on the side of maintaining too much of the traditional. Finally, they feared that the modern Koranic schools —instead of serving as a temporary substitute until enough Franco-Arab schools were built—would, by a sort of Gresham's

* The 1908 Congress represented perhaps the apogee of Young Tunisian influence on French opinion. Almost a dozen Young Tunisians, including Bechir Sfar and Abdel Djelil Zaouche, presented papers. It is an interesting comment on the development of the two countries to note that although Tunisia was represented by this strong delegation, the much larger Algerian native population, colonized for a full half-century longer, had only a single delegate.

law of education, replace the Franco-Arab schools altogether.

Again it is clear that ideologically they were true revolutionaries. Keenly aware of the cultural gap between modern Western and Arabic-Islamic societies, they knew that the only way to catch up was to make a sharp break with much of the past and to build anew on different foundations.

In a certain sense, however, Khairallah took a philosophical position more radical than that of his Young Tunisian critics. The latter never attacked Islamic principles head on; they merely ignored them, and concentrated on the practical needs of a different type of education. But Khairallah, in his report to the 1908 Congress, admitted the existence of a universal morality differing from Islamic morality, though he refrained from indicating which was more valid. He argued that his modern Koranic schools must teach not only Islamic morals but also, "since morality forms today a science resting on certain, immutable, obligatory rules which all men must respect, it must be taught as well, as an essential part of the program and not just as an accessory." He then concluded: "The children will thus have, on the one hand, the religious morality resting on the promises of reward and threats of punishment in a future life; on the other hand, the lay morality having its sanction in the conscience and public opinion. They will be able to choose later from one or the other their own rules of conduct."[13]

It can be seen, half a century later, that both sides were partly right. The modern Koranic schools, which by the end of the Protectorate period had one student for every four in the governmental Franco-Arab schools, did less to prepare students intellectually and psychologically for the modern world. These schools also became a major weapon of all those who were resisting Westernization and modernization. On the other hand, such a halfway house was needed for most of Tunisian society. But the real leadership, from the era of the Young Tunisians to the present, has continued to come from the French and Franco-Arab schools. The Young Tunisians were right in insisting on the policy of nothing but the best in education. As Bach Hamba puckishly observed, even Khairallah sent his children to the Lycée Carnot or the Lycée Jules Ferry (for girls).[14]

The Critical Faculty and the Absence of Apologetics

In a country ruled by an alien power, the daily confrontation with the colonial situation can be painful and even humiliating. The inescapable contrast between the small alien group—efficient, powerful, and confident—and the native group—subordinate, inefficient, and confused—must be faced and explained. It is not unnatural that such explanations often include a heavy dose of fiction to alleviate the pain—"Our society has more solidly based spiritual values," or "We were once greater than the colonizing power, and it was we who taught them the elements of civilization," or "This experience is God's punishment for our having departed from the true religion. We must return to the fundamentals." Such rationalizations do more, however, than alleviate the pain; they often obscure the nature of the illness. A society facing the problem of ideological readjustment must acknowledge the facts in order to change them.

The Young Tunisians seemed to enjoy turning a strong light on the weaker points in their own society as a preface to suggestions for change: "The Moslems of Tunisia are indolent, improvident, and fatalistic. They must be prodded into activity." "Traditional education is hopelessly outdated." "Tunisian secular justice is disorganized and inefficient." "Arabic as an instrument of modern, scientific education is inadequate," etc.

Although abused by a rightist colon party flaunting its alleged racial and cultural superiority, the Young Tunisians never let themselves be deflected from what they wanted from French civilization. The contributions that the French language and culture, French administration, even the French colon, had rendered were accepted, even extolled. Were they merely toadying to the French authorities? Such a question could stem only from a misreading of their program. The Young Tunisians were not a political party. They were an elite trying to interpret a new ideology to their countrymen while showing the French that a "policy of association" to modernize Tunisia was possible. They presented the ideas borrowed from an alien culture as attractively as possible only because they themselves believed in these ideas. The speech of Mohammed Lasram before the Sadiki alumni, an all-Tunisian audience, was not window dressing to please the French Resident General; it expressed a faith. The Young Tunisians, he affirmed, "will pursue their apostleship, under the aegis of France, with no concern other than to liberate their coreligionists from all prejudices that shackle their evolution, destroy their faculties, and hold them outside the movement that irresistibly carries humanity toward progress."[15]

The Young Tunisians never pretended that their program was a return to a golden age of Tunisian or Islamic history, "What good would it do Moslems of the twentieth century," argued Zaouche, "to return to the civilization of their ancestors if they had to remain strangers to scientific progress? Have the Italians simply restored Roman civilization, and are the Greeks content, like the Athenians of old, to cultivate the arts and philosophy?"[16] These men were too absorbed in the practical requirements of their immediate program either to need myths or to waste time in creating them.

The Young Tunisians were worthy heirs to the work begun by Kheireddine Pasha, and their writings and activities from roughly 1896 to 1912 constituted an ideology and a plan of action that, though buffeted from time to time by antagonists in the French community and local conservatives, eventually prevailed in an independent Tunisia.

The immediate cause of the demise of the Young Tunisian movement was a surprisingly small incident. They had supported, although not originated, a boycott of the Tunis tramlines, to last until the lines assured equal pay to Moslem employees and better treatment of Tunisian passengers by the Italian employees of the trams. After one month, the Protectorate Government imposed a solution by fiat. The Young Tunisians protested. On March 13, 1912, the Protectorate Government arrested seven Young Tunisian leaders and deported four of them. A few months later, martial law was imposed; it was not lifted until 1921.

This incident was really only the final step in an unfortunate process of declining mutual faith. The continued strident attacks of the *colon* party had set the stage. Following the Ottoman *rapprochement* with Germany, the Italian aggression against the Ottoman Empire in neighboring Libya in 1911, and, finally, the regrettable Djellaz incident* in Tunis in November of that same year—almost any pretext could have caused a break. The Young Tunisian movement, like that of Kheireddine, seemed to collapse rather ignominiously. In both cases, however, the ideas that had been intelligently and frankly advanced were destined to survive the temporary setback. After World War I, Tunisia would move into the third stage of the colonial situation.

* The Djellaz incident was a riot provoked by Moslem fear and mistrust about alleged plans of the municipality to confiscate a Moslem cemetery and by the government's mishandling of the cemetery affair, as well as by the arrogance of members of the Italian community in Tunis after the Ottoman-Italian war began.

4. Stage Three:
The Era of the Old Destour

In 1912, with the exile of the Young Tunisian leaders, came an abrupt end to the period of ideological formulation by an elite conscious of its intermediate position between protector and protégé. In 1919, a mass national organization sprang up almost overnight. This span of seven years divides the second and third stages of Tunisia's colonial experience.

There is little that can be said about Tunisian development during these years. For Tunisia, as for most of the world, the major fact of this period was World War I, which was tearing apart the nations on the other side of the Mediterranean. And even if the Tunisians and French in Tunisia had been willing to continue the debate that had so completely absorbed their attention a few years earlier, martial law, in effect from 1912 to 1921, stifled all but the most innocuous criticism.

Yet the influence of World War I on Tunisian ideological development was great, as it was in most other colonized states. The war hastened the collapse of the old traditional society; to the 100,000 Tunisians serving in France in the army or in work battalions, it brought both hardship (40,000 casualties) and rising expectations. It served to break down the mystique of an all-powerful West, for standards of administration declined when the more competent officials were called into military service, and there was less reason to be awed by a culture that seemed bent on self-annihilation. In addition, the lofty ideals of "Wilsonism" and the general European desire for a new order—whether democratic, pacifist, Communist, or fascist—spread to the colonial world, bringing with them the feeling that it was time for a change. Typical examples of this feeling were the attempt by a self-constituted Tunisian body to get a hearing at the Paris Peace

Conference, and the publication in Paris in 1920 of an anonymous book setting forth the Tunisian nationalists' claims.

The most important consequence of the war was the emergence of the Destour (Constitution) Party, organized in February, 1920, which grew into a national body able to claim the support of the majority of the Tunisian people. Like the Egyptian Wafd of the same period, it was a loose coalition of a number of not entirely reconcilable elements. For a time it was hardly respectable *not* to be a member of the Destour, and for just this reason, no political maneuver among Tunisians was acceptable without the Destour cachet. Although the party was more nearly the political and social portrait of an age than an apparatus for positive change, it was, despite its limitations, the major social and political fact of the 1920's. Its internal contradictions were legion: It was a "radical" group in the demands it made on the French, including independence, yet it was socially and politically conservative. It was the first modern mass political party in Tunisia, but had little sense of organizational activity. It could claim national support, yet it certainly did not faithfully represent all the various interests in Tunisia, particularly the economically underprivileged and those classes being created or expanded by the colonial situation.

If one compares the Old Destour Party with the later Neo-Destour, which grew out of it, one could say that the former was Islamic, traditionalist, socially reactionary, and inflexible, and the latter Western, secular, progressive, socially revolutionary, and flexible. But although there is much truth in these generalizations, by no means all the members of the Old Destour wore traditional dress, graduated from Zitouna University, and thought of nationalism in terms of an Arabic and Islamic framework. Nor did all the Neo-Destourians fit an Afro-Mediterranean form of the French Radical Socialists. Both groups evolved within an Arabic-Islamic framework and reacted to the stimuli of intruding Westernism. The Neo-Destour grew, after all, quite naturally out of the old party. One returns, inevitably, to the question of time and of stages of development: This was the third stage of Tunisia's colonial period, and this very fact goes far to explain both the strengths and the weaknesses of the Old Destour.

The party was a fortuitous, spontaneous, and somewhat surprising combination of those elements influenced by the earlier Young Tunisian movement and a much more broadly based traditional urban leadership. There was, in fact, a certain interchange of the terms "Young Tunisian" and "Destourian" in the first years. The adjectives "fortuitous" and "spontaneous" are used advisedly. Like the Egyptian Wafd (which means literally "delegation"), the Destour started as a group of self-appointed "lawyers" bent on arguing their brief before any "court" that might have jurisdiction—whether President Wilson, the Paris Peace Conference, or the Quai d'Orsay. It was the more or less spontaneous, and somewhat surprising, response of the unconsulted clients—the Tunisian people—that turned this "delegation" into a political party. It is quite likely that Taalbi and his supporters expected to follow in the tradition of the Young Tunisians, acting as intermediaries between their own people and the colonizing power, but the popular response—and here the catalyzing influence of World War I is important—converted the group into a political party. In a sense, therefore, the Old Destour had a double base—the small group carrying out, in modified circumstances, the earlier Young Tunisian idea of advocate and interlocutor, and the spontaneous mass movement that flowed naturally toward the existing, traditional leadership. The Old Destour bore traces of this double origin to the end.

One facet of this double origin was a tendency toward legalism. This formalism fitted both the social philosophy and the habitual caution and avoidance of total commitment of the traditional leadership. For this reason, the Westernized elite was content to present its brief to Paris, to frame its programs in terms of a constitution, to call in two French legal experts to maintain that the pre-Protectorate Tunisian constitution of 1861 was still valid,[1] and to plot its political actions in terms of the sort of brief that would be presented at the next round of negotiations. Like a good lawyer concerned with defending rather than reforming his client, the Westernized elite of the Old Destour accepted Tunisian society as they found it. The reforming zeal of Bach Hamba and Zaouche was now submerged in the desire to win the case. The group rested its case once every legal resort was exhausted, just as the lawyer's function ends after the last appeal has been made.

The legal comparison might seem both exaggerated and irrelevant, but two important facts should not be forgotten. First, this was the age of the Kellogg-Briand Pact, an age in which the thinking of the whole Western world was legalistic and formalistic. For most of the world, not yet fully awake to the forces of change exemplified by Communism and fascism, this was the heyday of liberal nationalism. Constitutions, self-determination, and a host of political rights became legitimate ends—not merely means.

In Tunisia, this largely Western-inspired formalistic legalism was matched and supported by the attitudes of the traditional society. The leaven of change brought by the Protectorate was working rapidly, but nevertheless in the 1920's, the leading citizens in Tunis, and even more so those in other towns and villages, lagged far behind the bold commitment to modernism found among the Young Tunisians. The Old Destour has been described by some Western observers as the party of this traditionalist Tunisian bourgeoisie, but this terminology perhaps obscures as much as it explains. It was neither the revolutionary bourgeoisie described by Marx, ushering in a dynamic, technical society, nor a bourgeoisie evoking images of Babbitt or characters of Stendhal, Flaubert, or Galsworthy. The mantle of leadership in Tunisia's first national political party fell upon a distinctive Islamic social class, a class that has no equivalent in Western terms.

Like medieval Islamic society in general, this class was urban-centered, but it was not the instrument of a commercial, industrial, or any other kind of revolution. It included the following: the religious leadership, or ulema; the religio-judicial leadership, or muftis, *caïds*, and *aduls* (notaries); prominent merchants; leaders of the most respected crafts; and the informal leaders of various quarters of the cities. This traditional group was the most self-contained and thus the least open to Western influence.

By contrast, the aristocracy had a long tradition of contact with European diplomats and businessmen even before the Protectorate, and the working class—both rural and urban—had had an increasing amount of direct contact with Europeans during the steady growth of the European community under the Protectorate.

La Tunisie Martyre, published in Paris after the hopes of the would-be Tunisian delegates to the Peace Conference were dashed, is in many ways the political testament of the Old Destour. This work of Sheik Taalbi and Ahmed Sakka, with the collaboration of a few other Tunisians, is of above-average quality as a compilation of factual data placed in the framework of a political polemic. One major premise of this book separates the Old Destour from the earlier Young Tunisian movement as well as from the later Neo-Destour—the concept of a golden age that allegedly existed before the Protectorate. Before 1881, the book argues, there was a constitution, a representative assembly, a free society, and a thriving economy. The French Protectorate completely changed that. Although the very use of statistics in the book bears witness to the influence of Western ideas, the basic emotional theme is that of a desire to get back to the "good old days."

Le Tunisien had started publication with the platform that a generation had passed and the modernizing work of the Protectorate was beginning to bear fruit, thanks to the impact of French culture. *La Tunisie Martyre,* on the other hand, insisted that Tunisia had wanted a national, scientific education, but that all she got was French education—as foreign to Tunisia as Chinese education would be to France.[2] Later, the Neo-Destour, while rejecting assimilation as an affront to national dignity, still insisted that French socialist and liberal ideas be applied in a manner appropriate to Tunisia. *La Tunisie Martyre,* however, merely wanted to recapture an alleged paradise lost. Admittedly, the concluding pages listed specific recommendations very much in the tradition of Western liberal nationalism—a legislature, local government, an independent judiciary, free and compulsory primary education—but the basic theme was that Tunisia must recover what she had possessed before the Protectorate. This was more than just a tactical weapon to embarrass the colonizing power into granting Tunisians more participation in government. When William Jennings Bryan spoke of crucifying mankind on a cross of gold, he was engaging in absurd hyperbole, but the basic idea of an easy credit policy was well understood by both partisans and opponents. Similarly, the idea of a well-ordered society existing before 1881 was an effective emotional symbol to all those Tunisians who, faced with a revolutionary change from static to dynamic society, wanted only to withdraw and retrench.

It must be remembered that the Taalbi of *La Tunisie Martyre* was the same man who had collaborated in writing *L'Esprit Libéral du Coran* less than a generation earlier. He had then insisted in his plea for Franco-Moslem cooperation that "the Moslem, by studying the sources of his religion, is capable of acquiring corrective ideas which must necessarily modify his education and his mentality and must make for you [French] a devoted collaborator, capable of affection, of entire submission [*sic*], and of absolute confidence."[3] Does this mean that Taalbi had a complete change of heart once he became a political leader? Or was he something of a hypocrite? In the same way, the French-language newspaper of the Old Destour, *Le Libéral*, had as its motto "Organe de Collaboration Franco-Tunisienne," but the Arabic-language press of the same party took a much less "collaborating" line.

These instances reflect the traditional mentality of large sectors of the Old Destour and of a society whose members did not exteriorize their innermost thoughts. The most important interactions took place within the family, basic principles were settled and not subject to discussion, and public life occupied a narrow and somewhat secondary field. Although form was not necessarily more important than substance, since the substance was basically unquestioned, form was the only area left for the free play of individual talent. The literature of the traditional society was more evocative than rational: It was a language of symbol, syllogism, and simile—utterly foreign to Cartesian doubt, Pascalian introspection, Romantic self-expression, or Bergsonian evolutionism—and it is therefore not surprising that the traditional literary style produced no novels, no autobiography, no drama, and no free verse.

As a corollary, public utterances and writings were more often a performance than a serious debate of principles. In Western terms, the political polemics were always on the level of tactics because the more basic tenets were merely assumed. Thus, Taalbi could equate the Koran with the principles of the French Revolution in one book and condemn the extension of French culture in Tunisia in another. In each he was defending *his* side, the Tunisian Moslem society. He was *not* committing his inner self in this external argument. Therefore, neither he nor his more traditional readers would feel that he had changed his fundamental position.

The attitude of the writers in *Le Libéral,* who had a basically French education, illustrates the legalistic approach of the Old Destour. Although the Western-dressed Destourian was no longer traditional in his thinking, he could nevertheless easily justify his position by seeing himself as a lawyer looking after the interests of his client.

The Old Destour was a national party with local organizations in various towns and villages. The main leadership, however, came from the old Tunis families and a few outsiders who had established themselves in the capital, often after an education at Zitouna University. This combination—"Tunisois" and old families—gave the Old Destour leadership a certain myopia, which contributed to its easy overthrow by the Neo-Destour in the next decade. The leaders ignored or underestimated the rise of a wage-earning urban proletariat and a new intelligentsia of modest social origins created by the Franco-Arab schools and Sadiki College. And they were virtually unaware of the changes in agriculture produced by the settling down of the nomads and the advent of capitalistic farming. Nor did they usually realize that the small craftsman making *chechias* (the red Tunisian fez), the perfume merchant in the old *medina,* and the teacher in a *kuttab* were becoming outmoded unfortunates rather than members of prestigious professions.

Thus, not only was the Old Destour created almost overnight, but it started life with the liability of deriving its main support from groups declining daily in power and prestige. This is not to deny that it "represented" Tunisia in the mid-1920's, but in situations of rapid social change, it is sometimes necessary to look for smaller groups, or for ideas not yet completely accepted by any large party, in order to locate the influences that are determining the way the society will move. Let us now consider these other factors influencing social change.

FACTORS INFLUENCING SOCIAL CHANGE

The Continuing Idea of Dynamic Reform

The period of the Old Destour marked a certain step backward from the more daring reformist program of the Young Tunisians, but this was inevitable as political activity shifted from the Tunisian elite to the masses. "Islah" was now everybody's motto, with even the most ardent conservatives insisting on their own brand of reform. This reforming spirit was often intimately linked with a highly developed sense of self-criticism. A Tunisian who later held important high office, Mohamed Saleh Mzali, insisted in 1921, "If a country does not evolve, it remains in a state of intellectual, moral, and economic dependence in relation to more advanced countries."[4] He listed the seven major obstacles to progress in Tunisia, among them fatalism and improvidence, ignorance of economic facts, lack of order and regularity, and "Byzantinism."* This last fault, Mzali observed, "is found espe-

---

* This critical self-examination and drive for reform came from other, quite different sources. Interestingly, it took on at times an almost puritanical rigor, as witness the articles in the short-lived Communist newspaper *Habib al Umma:* "The present competition will not permit us a moment's rest. Let us abandon resignation, for a *hadith* [saying of the Prophet] has said, 'Work for this world as if you were to live forever.' Let us view our status as it is, not as we suppose it was in the past." (October 25, 1921.) A later article also scored Byzantinism and ostentatious wealth, which, it warned, usually leads to impoverishment. (October 31, 1921.) The author was Othman Kaak, currently director of the Bibliothèque Nationale. Like many other writers for this Communist paper, Kaak seemed much more interested in a search for a new "idea of change" than in Communism itself.

cially among the educated Tunisians. It is characterized by the taste for sterile discussion, love of useless chatter, of discussions based on equivocal words which are admired more for their false ingenuity than for their direct activity. The origin of this must be found in juridical and religious discussions pushed to their extreme limit and in the often unnecessary studies which Arabic education frequently delights in."[5]

Even *La Tunisie Martyre* felt a need to score "Byzantinism." In a reference to the many cultural influences that had shaped Tunisia, the book maintained that the Byzantines had brought only "luxury and prodigality," while the Arabs brought "religion, the keen sense of justice, fraternity, equality, democracy, science, letters, and the arts."[6]

Perhaps the most biting social criticism came from Tahar Haddad, the rebel par excellence of the 1920's. Born into a modest family in Tunis, in 1899, Tahar Haddad had a thoroughly traditional education. Yet in spite of, or perhaps because of, this, he was to symbolize the extreme revolutionary attack not only against imperialism, but even more against the traditional framework of his own society. A trade unionist and journalist, he is now best remembered for two important and provocative books. The first, *The Tunisian Workers and the Appearance of a Trade-Union Movement*,[7] created something of a scandal by leaving off the traditional invocation of God's mercy at the beginning of the book. The second, *Our Women in the Sharia and in Society*,[8] was a thoroughgoing plea for women's rights. It became a *cause célèbre* and resulted in his dismissal from Zitouna University. Public criticism coupled with repudiation by former associates probably contributed to his early death four years later. The lonely figure of Tahar Haddad, apparently an almost pathological pessimist, appears time and again in every social history of Tunisia in the post-World War I decade. His role, like that of a Tom Paine or a George Bernard Shaw, was to provoke controversy and thus jar people out of their long unquestioned beliefs. In the Tunisia of today, he is perhaps praised excessively, but his part in turning the Tunisian toward modernism was considerable.

Criticizing the existing society, Haddad placed his arguments for dynamic change within a Marxist framework: "From these jolts given by European colonization there grew up once more among Tunisians a movement of activity and emulation. Thus they learned the significance of land which had lain fallow and they learned that its economic value lay in its productivity, not merely in its ownership."[9] Haddad thought the class struggle had no meaning for Tunisia, since the colonizing power had impoverished all elements of the indigenous society; the struggle was rather between native society and the colonizing capitalists supported by the Protectorate Government.

The puritan streak, that strange disgust at "Byzantinism," also came out in Haddad's writings. He scorned the urban upper class, who disliked working with their hands, and pointed out how some disliked trades as well, since that involved "catering to customers, showing wares, and even in some cases, handling heavy things." Some families, he observed ironically, got around this drawback "by dealing in precious things such as perfume and by the manufacture of *chechias* in the deep shade under heavy roofs giving protection from the heat of the sun and the cold of the rain."[10] Other classes of Tunisians fared little better with Haddad, including the fellah, who might work hard for a while, but without foresight or planning.

Another source of reformist zeal was the small Parti Réformiste, created in 1921. Composed of dissidents from the Old Destour, many of whom were directly connected with the earlier Young Tunisians, this party also conducted a campaign for change, rejecting the "golden age" myth and insisting on a bit of self-reform as well. In fact, their platform might almost be summed up as a commitment to modernization in large measure *à la française*. Yet this small movement was insignificant, scorned and even hated by large elements of the population. Perhaps one can see the Parti Réformiste as a group of now obsolete Young Tunisians. It was time to move on to a mass organization, but they continued to think in terms of educating their own people while winning concessions from the French through moderation and good behavior. Such a stand at this point showed both a certain lack of faith in the masses and an unwillingness to risk anything in the struggle for modernization.

Thus, the ideas of reform, dynamism, and self-criticism were in the air in this period, reaching beyond the limited scope of a small elite. For a time, the conservatism of the Old Destour would restrain the more dynamic ideas of modernization. But it was clear that if the various divided proponents of change—the graduates of French and Franco-Arab schools in Tunisia, those returning from their studies in France, the rising urban proletariat, the agricultural workers, the small group of social critics, and the Westernized elements of the old aristocracy—could all be brought together, the future would be theirs. This happened eventually with the creation of the Neo-Destour, but first several other obstacles had to be removed or at least radically changed.

The "New" European Influence—The French Socialists

The large European community in Tunisia had always played an important role in breaking down the old society and pointing the way toward a new one. The *colon* with his modern agricultural methods, the technician, the schoolteacher, the administrator, the industrialist, even the large number of unveiled, emancipated women often working outside the home, were ever-present representatives of the modern world. However, as seems to happen inexorably in the colonial situation, the relations between protectors and protégés, never intimate, grew even more strained in this period. To avoid a virtual segregation of the two groups, some continuing point of contact was required. Earlier, there had been the close relationship between the Young Tunisians and various liberal French circles in Tunisia and in metropolitan France. Now, however, with the beginning of mass political organization in Tunisia, a contact solely between well-intentioned liberals on the one hand and a small aristocracy rapidly declining in prestige on the other would be inadequate, if not actually harmful.

It was the French Socialists and the trade-union movement that provided this necessary link in the post-World War I period.

The Socialists in Tunisia were never a very large group, with an official membership of a few hundred at the most.[11] The trade-union movement, linked with the French Confédération Générale des Travailleurs (CGT), had a membership of only a little more than 40,000 at the peak. But their leadership was active and vocal, and their views of society appealed to the Tunisians. At a time when almost all political, social, and economic activity followed ethnic lines, the Socialist movement transcended race and religion. In the early days of organizing their movement, when the Old Destour leaders were inclined to sharpen the dichotomy between "us" (the Tunisians) and "them" (the French and other Europeans), the Socialists alone criticized institutions both of their own French society and of traditional Tunisian society. Since a major difficulty for any colonized society is to avoid rejecting indiscriminately all aspects of the culture of the colonizing power, the existence of a group like the French Socialists was extremely important. For if Frenchmen could accept part of their own cultural tradition while violently opposing other parts, obviously the Tunisians could be equally eclectic without damaging their own national identity.

Nationalism in any form was the major enemy of the Socialists of Tunisia. They were equally critical of the pretensions of the *colon* party and what they termed the xenophobic religious fanaticism of the Destour. They argued that both France and Tunisia suffered from the same plight—the dominance of capitalists and clergy—and that in both countries it was the dead hand of tradition that made these forces so powerful. Their solution was to liberate minds from past superstition and error, and then to organize the masses into trade unions and political structures to take over power held by the capitalist class and the religious institution. Sometimes, admittedly, the Socialists hedged on this program, foreseeing a rather long period of tutelage for the Tunisians, but they remained for the most part true to their principles. They made an effort to recruit members of all races into their organizations, and both the Section Française de l'Internationale Ouvrière (SFIO) and the CGT had French, Italians, Jews, Maltese, and Tunisian Moslems in their ranks. The

Socialists can also take most of the credit for the recognition in 1936 of the principle of "equal work, equal pay."

Largely because of Socialist influence, Tunisian nationalism was forced to justify itself in more universal moral terms. Joachim Durel, long a teacher at the Lycée Carnot and one of the most active Socialists in Tunisia, could praise the beginnings of the trade-union movement in 1924 with the observation that it was time the Arab, French, and Italian workers learned they all belonged to the same country and were "all harnessed to the same water wheel."[12] What was needed in Tunisia was an antidote to the excesses of racial nationalism—French or Tunisian—and this the Socialists provided. Because of their efforts, both the Tunisian nationalist and trade-union movements grew in an environment that compelled them to reiterate that their organizations were not based on any idea of racial or religious exclusiveness. The Socialists were equally severe with the Catholic Church. They attacked, for instance, the erection of a statue of Cardinal Lavigerie brandishing the cross at the entrance to the old *medina* in Tunis, and challenged the wisdom of holding the Eucharistic Congress at Carthage in 1931. The Socialists made it more difficult for Tunisians to lump together the Church and the French Protectorate, and thus they helped to prevent the colonial struggle from taking the shape of an Islamic-Christian battle.

The Socialists in Tunisia were also strong supporters of female emancipation, recognizing it as a necessary step toward effective modernization. In traditional Moslem societies, women were uneducated and barred from any sort of social life to such an extent that linguists could isolate distinct female dialects in most Arab countries. Tunisian society in the 1920's was probably some twenty or thirty years behind that of Egypt and the Levant. Even the Young Tunisians, for all their Western and liberal sympathies, had hedged on this issue, being content with a passing gesture in favor of more female education. In effect, anyone tackling this problem in Tunisia faced a formidable task. For a long time, it was only the Socialists and a handful of Tunisian Moslems closely connected with them who faced the issue at all. The Socialist position was spearheaded by Mme. Eva Fichet, alias Eve Nohelle, the wife of a Socialist in Tunisia and the sister of an even more active Socialist, André Duran-Angliviel. Through her Tunisian branch of the Ligue des Femmes pour la Paix et la Liberté, where almost no women but a sprinkling of Tunisian Moslem men and a handful of liberal young Frenchmen gathered to debate current issues, as well as through personal contact and articles in *Tunis Socialiste,* Mme. Fichet exerted a strong influence in favor of women's rights.*

Socialist influence can also be readily detected in other issues eventually adopted by the Neo-Destour and the independent Tunisian Government: the emphasis on the role of trade-unionism, national economic planning, lay education, the abolition of *habous,* and a generally liberal, universalist approach to international problems.

It is important to note the sympathetic relations between the French Socialists and the young Tunisian nationalists. Durel had occasion to answer Tahar Haddad's charge that the French Socialists were the dominators just like the *colons* and other Rightists in Tunisia.

"Yes," retorted Durel with heavy-handed irony, "it is always the Frenchman who is the enemy. . . . That rapacious and slothful feudalism which you have suffered for centuries and which has fabricated in you the souls of slaves, that mosque in whose shadow you eternalize your intellectual servitude and that 'glorious past' whose delusion suffocates and empoisons you—these real causes of your misery and your downfall you do not want to see. It will be necessary, however, to choose between the slow but sure death in the abject poverty of your old traditions and a renewed life in a grand effort of intelligence and of collaboration with men of the West."[13]

One might think that this was scarcely designed to bring Tunisians to accept Durel's thesis. Yet, in a real sense, the Durel approach—typical of that of the Socialists in Tunisia—was much more sympathetic and effective than one careful to avoid any discussion that might offend the *indigène.* For Durel and the other Socialists in Tunisia showed their deep concern with the problems

* *Tunis Socialiste* was one of the very few sources to defend Tahar Haddad when his book advocating female emancipation as consistent with Islam caused a storm in Zitouna circles.

of their Tunisian colleagues and opponents, and they also placed their own convictions squarely in view. They discussed the issues with the Tunisians, face to face, without hedging. Since the major fear of the Tunisian nationalists in this period was that they would be completely absorbed into the French political structure, they might well have been tempted to gloss over their own domestic problems but for the brutal frankness of the Socialists.

In reviewing the press of the time, one gets the impression that, generally speaking, the Socialists came off best in the arguments with the Old Destour, but when Bourguiba and his colleagues first entered the fray in the 1930's, the Tunisian nationalists did well indeed in the debate. The Socialist dialectic (not so much in the Marxist as in the original Greek sense of the term) had left its imprint on Tunisian ideological development.

The First Indigenous Trade-Union Movement

Without the Socialists and their CGT, the first Tunisian trade-union movement would probably have come into existence much later than it did and would have taken quite a different form. But their were two other groups that were also active during the period of strikes and organizing that led to the founding of the first indigenous trade-union organization. One of them revolved around the quixotic figure of Mohammed Ali.* Born about 1895

* The details of Mohammed Ali's life before and after his work in Tunisia in 1924–25 are somewhat hazy. It is known that he left for Tripoli at the time of the Italo-Turkish War, and from there moved on to Egypt and Turkey. Toward the end of World War I, he allegedly studied economics at Berlin University, and received a degree in the early 1920's. Within a year after his return to Tunisia in 1924, his activities had led to his arrest, and in November, 1925, he was sentenced to ten years' banishment from Tunisia. He left for Egypt and was soon working as chauffeur for a "grand pasha" in Cairo, where he apparently lost his job for disobeying his employer's orders to drive the French ambassador in Cairo home from a reception. (Cf. Habib Bourguiba, *La Tunisie et la France* [Paris, 1954], p. 382.) He was working as a driver between Jedda and Mecca in Saudi Arabia when he was killed in 1932 in an automobile accident. Fortunately, the most important aspect of Mahammed Ali's career is fairly well documented, and from the critical coverage of both the French Rightist and Socialist press, balanced by the sympathetic and detailed book by Tahar Haddad, it is possible to re-create with some assurance his activities of this time.

near Gabès in southern Tunisia, Mohammed Ali spent several adventurous years in the Middle East and Europe before he returned to Tunisia in 1924 and threw himself into an unsuccessful scheme for organizing consumer cooperatives. In mid-August, the dockers of Tunis went on strike. Mohammed Ali and his small following were quick to offer their services. They moved from strike to strike—from Tunis to Bizerte. Some of the strikes were settled with at least a few concessions on the part of the employers, and the conviction grew among the Tunisian workers that the time had come to act, that something could now be accomplished. Mohammed Ali's support of the Tunis dockers certainly triggered the movement for an indigenous trade-union organization.

The third group jockeying for position was a small Communist one—partly French and partly Tunisian—openly working to create a trade-union organization that would belong to the Third International. Tahar Haddad admits that the Communists had hopes of swallowing up the Tunisian workers' organization, but he insists they were bound to fail, as their idea of class war had no meaning in "colonies" like Tunisia. The unions being created would be concerned with more than just raising wages. They were to act as clubs for education in trades and agriculture, leading eventually toward a situation when, with an accumulation of capital, they could move into a sort of producers' cooperative.[14]*

All this activity led to the creation, in December, 1924, of the first indigenous and autonomous trade-union organization, the Confédération Générale des Travailleurs Tunisiens (CGTT). It

---

* This idea of the trade union as a club merits further examination. As in most of the Arab world, many of the Tunisian crafts and employments were organized along lines of special racial or regional groupings (Djerbans as retail grocers; Metouia, from a small town near Gabès, as dock workers; Andalusians as craftsmen of *chechias;* Jewish tailors; etc.). At the same time, members of the same craft or industry tended to belong to the same religious brotherhood. Certainly, much of the emotional appeal of unionism in 1924 stemmed from this fraternal feeling. It has even been suggested that the transition went something as follows: In 1924, a man was a member of his brotherhood first and the trade union second, but by 1945, a man was trade-unionist (or, for that matter, a Neo-Destourian) first, and the brotherhood tie was definitely secondary.

proved to be a short-lived confederation, for the Protectorate Government soon showed its intention to cripple, or at the very least harass, the new organization. When two new strikes broke out, one in a cement factory and the other among agricultural workers on a large estate, Mohammed Ali moved to give the CGTT active support. The government soon found cause to arrest him on charges of conspiracy against the state. Deprived of its leader and rejected by all groups, both indigenous and French, the CGTT soon dissolved.

The Socialists argued that the creation of the CGTT was a step backward, that trade-union unity had been split by the creation of a group whose *raison d'être* was religious and nationalistic. On the other hand, it is more likely that the short-lived CGTT advanced the cause of modernization, since it spread the idea of trade-unionism to groups that had been only slightly touched by the efforts of the CGT. It also gave the Tunisians some experience in organizing and maintaining a union on their own, without outside help. Finally, it provoked the CGT into a realization that Tunisian labor was not an inert force to be paternalistically guided and taken for granted.

Whatever may have been the outlook of the CGTT rank and file, the essentially modern orientation of Mohammed Ali and his small clique—especially Tahar Haddad—is indisputable. In his discussions with workers, Mohammed Ali stressed that if Tunisians boasted of their strength while in their present state, they would only increase French contempt. He urged Tunisian workers to set their own house in order and restore their strength and pride; then "we would be able to convince a large number of French and Europeans that we deserve to attain a life of freedom just like them."[15] Tahar Haddad summed up the philosophy of the CGTT: Any group or nation must build up its own strength. It cannot rely on some outside force "whether it be a state, a political party, or a private group." Tunisia was not yet in a position to enter into a cooperation of equals. She must accept outside assistance, but it was essential "to guard the freedom of thought and action in accordance with the plan the country has decided for herself and by herself."[16] Thus, Tunisia needed, among other things, her own autonomous trade-union organization.

The CGTT claimed to be based on a more perfect fulfillment of the aims of the CGT. Haddad readily conceded the strong influence of the European workers in Tunisia and of the CGT in leading the Tunisian workers to "break away from their past history of being content with the ordained state of affairs."[17] He maintained, however, that the Tunisians who had joined unions affiliated with the CGT had found prejudice and discrimination in the midst of an organization that claimed to be based on the idea of the equality and cooperation of all workers, and for this reason, they tended to abandon the CGT. The CGTT—prodded, of course, in large measure by Socialist attacks—insisted that it was open to all regardless of race or religion.

Finally, the CGTT—a basically native undertaking in a period when the Tunisians were still completely dominated by the foreign protector—was bound to have an impact as "myth" and inspiration for later activity. This is not the first time that an ignominious defeat has advanced a cause much better than a modest victory. When Ferhat Hached began his work of organizing his Union Générale des Travailleurs Tunisiens (UGTT) in 1944, he had two decades of Tunisian trade-union experience to build upon.

The Desacralization of Tunisian Society

At the end of the eighteenth century, when the dynamic, humanistic ideas of Western civilization began to disturb the medieval concept of an unchanging, divinely ordained society, a process was set in motion that would eventually force each affected society to reinterpret its religio-philosophical premises. The modalities of this reinterpretation, still being worked out by the various Islamic states and followed with great interest by all students of religious thought, probably provide the best key to a true understanding of any Islamic society today.

In general, any Moslem society faced with the problem of modernization would have three major alternatives: (1) the process of reinterpretation would accompany the various material changes and try to govern the acceptance of such changes; or (2) the material changes would be absorbed by the society without any real attempt being made to reconcile them with traditional dogma; or (3) the religious institutions of the society would be pushed aside, and the question of finding a new and acceptable reinterpretation would be, temporarily at least, subordinated to the problem of pragmatically adjusting to the material changes. Aside from the religious and moral implications of the three possibilities, it can be seen that from the viewpoint of ideological modernization, the first means would be cautious and conservative, always subject to the ultimate veto of the religious argument that any given innovation is "not consistent with religion." The second would involve a considerable degree of self-deception on the part of the whole society and could well lead to uneasy and irrational behavior as groups stumbled between the compartmented and unreconciled "old" and "new." The third possibility compares in part with what happened in Western civilization after the Reformation or, on a more restricted scale, with the temporary crisis of American Protestantism on the issue of Darwin's theory of evolution.

The reformist movement of Sheik Mohammed Abduh of Egypt represents the best example of the first alternative in modern Moslem society. That Abduh's disciple, Sheik Rashid Rida, died in 1935 an almost forgotten man is sufficient to indicate how completely the first alternative has been abandoned by most Islamic societies. In fact, much of the entire Moslem world today (with the exception of areas just beginning the process, such as Yemen) has opted for the second alternative, with perhaps some leanings toward the third.

The most clear-cut example of the third alternative is, of course, Turkey. Since her independence, Tunisia has appeared almost as bold, with the vital difference that the changes have been based on persuasion and public acceptance rather than on governmental fiat. The state of mind making possible this rapid postindependence adjustment had been developing since the time of Kheireddine Pasha, but the decisive period was that of the late 1920's and early 1930's. It was the adjustment reached during this time which insured that Tunisia's final stage of colonial development would take the form it did.

Most of the changes fostering this "desacralization"* have already been discussed, but it might be worthwhile to list them briefly again if only to note the imposing total impact: the increasing prestige of French lay education and concomitant decline of the traditional Zitouna education; the growing familiarity on all levels of society with daily change and the necessity of adaptation; the rise of secular jurisdiction and the decline of the Islamic Sharia courts; the subtle reshaping of old institutions, such as the transition from religious brotherhoods to trade unions. The shifting power base tended to leave the old religious leadership without authority: the fellah appealed directly to the French *contrôleur civil* instead of the *marabout* or the *caïd*, and to the French-trained *avocat* rather than the Moslem-trained mufti as the man to solve difficult legal problems, while the Western-trained doctor and pharmacist modified the former religious resignation in the face of sickness.

At the same time, the religious ulema in Tunisia made a very poor adjustment to the new world. The religious leadership never had a major reformer such as Sheik Mohammed Abduh of Egypt, and, even worse, almost all of the support in Tunisia for Sheik Abduh's movement came from outside the ulema circles. The Tunisian ulema is typified by Sheik Mohammed el Khider Hussein, who at the turn of the century was "leaning toward reform"[18] and, twenty years later, as rector of Al Azhar University in Egypt, had become the personification of religious conservatism.

In addition to being conservative and intellectually uninspired, Tunisian ulema of this period were also timid in their dealings with their French rulers. Most of their petitions to the govern-

---

* Both this term and the argument presented here reflect the influence of Jacques Berque, who has suggested that modern Arab society is in the process of passing from the "sacral" to the "historic." (Cf. his *Les Arabes d'Hier à Demain* [Paris, 1960].) This term is more satisfactory than "secularization," for by common usage what is "secular" is no longer "religious," but that which is "desacralized" is not necessarily deprived of religious content but is merely stripped of its taboo.

ment were designed to win perquisites for themselves; they were never closely identified with any indigenous reform or protest movement. The Khaldouniya was created in the face of religious opposition; most of the Zitouna University student strikes were directed in part against their own ulema and relied on outside support. When the Catholic Church organized the Eucharistic Congress in Carthage in 1931, the Sheik el Islam as well as the bey agreed to participate in the opening. This would have been appropriate if the ulema had been attempting to place Islam and Christianity on a footing of mutual respect, but this was not the case. They were merely bowing to authority.

Nevertheless, if the conservative religious hierarchy in Tunisia was vulnerable in the 1920's, it was still not to be defeated by frontal assault. This was the lesson of the severe reaction to Tahar Haddad's book *Our Women in the Sharia and in Society.** This incident underlined the way the religious authorities could exercise a powerful inhibiting influence—almost a power of veto —on any modernist movement. To a great extent, so long as the "high priestly authority" remained intact, any modernist movement remained exposed to the danger of sudden anathema, which could well mean loss of all political influence.

The modernists therefore set about the "desacralization" of Tunisia in a more indirect manner. Their flanking attack was the cautious theorizing that the religious institution should be "above" but not "outside" of many day-to-day problems, and the

---

* Haddad's belief that female emancipation was consistent with the principles of Islam, plus his more general idea that certain established points of Islamic dogma could and should be revised in the light of present-day experience, met with an attempt by the Council of Zitouna University to ban the book. When the government refused to go along, the Council had to be content with stripping Haddad of his degree and his right to teach at the Mosque-University. Several books "refuting" Haddad were quickly published by religious sheiks, and only a few intrepid Tunisians dared defend his thesis. In addition, Tunisian papers and magazines that had been cautiously pushing female rights soon dropped the subject. In fact, years later, after the achievement of female emancipation, a sensitive French observer wondered "if female emancipation would not have been realized more quickly and without disturbance if Tahar Haddad had not wished to justify it by an interpretation of the sacred texts." (Henri de Montéty, *Femmes de Tunisie* [Paris, 1958], p. 85.)

final coup was the campaign against naturalization, in 1933, in which they defended Islam but scored the religious hierarchy for dereliction of duty.

Patriotism was one method used to encroach on the domain of the religious and the "sacral" without directly opposing them. Under a well-developed doctrine of patriotism, religion is merely one of several factors of social solidarity. The author of an article in a series on the "Formation of the New Tunisian," in *L'Etendard Tunisien,* observed that it was basically this "new notion of the *patrie"* that explained the new Tunisian. Contrary to the customary opinion that Islam is both a religion and a nation, he wrote, the Tunisian feels at home only in Tunisia— although this is not to deny "the link attaching him to his co-religionists in other countries." A common language was also important, but something even more tangible constituted the *patrie:* common mores, needs, aspirations, and, especially, a common past. We are proud, the article continued, of our common past. "This small *patrie,* which has been so often profaned by the foreigner, which has known the alternatives of prosperity and misery, which has not—unfortunately—received its share of all the elements making for great richness, this *patrie* the new Tunisian loves with all the love of which he is capable, is devoted to it to the point of abnegation, all without ceasing to be faithful to the spirit of Islam."[19]

The patriotic motif was eminently flexible. One cannot lightly reinterpret religion, but a nation's history lends itself to many interpretations. Tunisians, as patriots, could take pride in Hannibal, St. Augustine, and Ibn Khaldoun. They could see Tunisia as an heir of the best of Mediterranean civilization, a theme that was to be extensively developed a decade later in the Arabic-language review *Al Mabahith.* Thus, according to the historical interpretation chosen, Tunisia could be Mediterranean and more closely identified with Europe, or Arab and move toward the East. The adoption of new ideas could be justified by recalling the many outside influences shaping Tunisia.

This is not to imply that the idea of patriotism was merely a tactical weapon in the hands of the modernists. R. P. André

Demeerseman, in his *Confession d'un Musulman,* has pointed
out how it fulfilled a real psychological need:

> The Tunisian intellectual of that period who participated in the
> Orient-Occident dialogue . . . began to experience metaphysical dis-
> array and pass through crises of doubt or skepticism. In the eyes of
> those who rejected such a discussion on principle, he had compromised
> himself by considering the possibilities of a conciliation between his
> Islamic heritage and his new culture. . . . From his disarray, patri-
> otism became the highest, the most stirring reason for living—in any
> case for a whole category of intellectuals.[20]

There was yet another way of de-emphasizing religion without either getting involved in an anticlerical stance or appearing
to suggest fundamental reinterpretations. This was to protect
religion from profane debasement by insisting that it should not
be invoked to cover all ordinary aspects of daily life. This argument amounted to the substitution of human reason for dogma
in all but the ultimate principles. The most stimulating presenta-
tion of this idea was made by Tahar Sfar in two articles on the
need for reforms at Zitouna University. Sfar made a bold claim
that this was the century of reason and science, and he spiked
the guns of orthodox conservatives with the demand that it
was therefore essential

> . . . not to extend in a fantastic manner the "sacred" to cover all the
> domain of the "known," under the pretext that this "known" has a
> relation, near or far, with the venerated texts. On the contrary, the
> sacred, that inviolable domain, must be reduced to the strictly neces-
> sary, to that which is essentially of divine origin and of which neither
> the source nor the intangibility can be a matter of doubt—a definition
> which to my mind applies only to the Koran and to the *hadiths*
> recognized and judged valid by the ancient authorities. [Only in this
> way] will the "sacred" be able to continue its socially beneficial role
> as a factor of stability, of order, and, above all, of morality, without
> the risk of suffocating scientific thought.[21]

Of course these ideas would not gain the approval of a traditional Moslem theologian; but although he could attack Tahar
Haddad for an attempted reinterpretation of the sacred texts,

he would find it difficult to oppose an argument that invoked reason, science, relativity, and dynamic and static religion, and at the same time affirmed the value of faith, the "sacral," and the sacred texts.

After the flanking movement, the "coup" was accomplished during the campaign against French naturalization. In 1923, the Protectorate Government passed a law giving Tunisian Moslems, among others, the right under certain conditions to obtain French citizenship. Although tangible benefits accrued to those who accepted French citizenship, only a handful of Tunisians took advantage of the legislation. The potentially strong reaction to this measure was vastly increased by the fact that it was placed in a religious context. Since the French Moslem would be judged by French civil courts and not by the Sharia in matters of personal status, it could be claimed that the naturalized citizen was an apostate.

The spark needed to touch off a campaign came in Bizerte in December, 1932. The mufti of Bizerte had given a *fatwa* (legal advisory opinion) that denied the right of burial in the Moslem cemetery to a recently deceased *naturalisé,* and an angry crowd of Moslems soon gathered at the cemetery to prevent his burial. Lines quickly hardened on both sides for a test of strength on this issue, the Tunisian cause being led by Habib Bourguiba's paper *L'Action Tunisienne.* The French Government was in no mood to compromise. The Protectorate authorities sought opinions from the leading Hanafi and Maliki ulema. The finding of the former group gave some satisfaction to the French, but only a small minority of Tunisians were of the Hanafi rite. The Maliki opinion given by Sheik Tahar Ben Achour, one of the most liberal and modern Tunisian ulema, did not satisfy either side. Ben Achour, obviously seeking a means of placating both sides and getting the problem off the front pages, stipulated that a *naturalisé* could "repent" his acceptance of French citizenship and be reintegrated into the Moslem faith. Bourguiba and his colleagues, however, knew that they had a good issue and had no intention of dropping the matter. *L'Action Tuni-*

sienne insisted that *naturalisés* could be buried only in separate cemeteries and suggested that all the "pusillanimous" ulema who had given in to the government on this vital question should resign.

The issue was made to order as a means of scoring the "governmental" ulema. Dr. Materi, later the first President of the Neo-Destour, noted that most of the *naturalisés* were poorly educated persons who did not fully realize the implications of accepting French citizenship. The ulema had been derelict in not making the religious error of naturalization clear to Moslems at the very beginning. All the ulema, he continued, privately admitted that a Moslem who voluntarily takes himself outside the Koranic law ceases to be a Moslem, and that the governmental edict against their advising others of this was no excuse for such an evasion of duty.[22] The paper also suggested that even if all of the ulema should announce in favor of French naturalization, it would make no difference, since the laws of Islam on this matter were clear and inescapable.[23]

After several incidents involving burial of *naturalisés* in the Moslem cemeteries under armed guard and their later clandestine exhumation, the government gave in and created special cemeteries for the *naturalisés*. Soon after, in May, 1933, the various Destourian newspapers were suspended and the Destour dissolved by the government. However, the real victory won in this naturalization campaign was indicated in a letter to *L'Action Tunisienne* of April 27, 1933, entitled "Our Revenge." An anonymous young Tunisian wrote that many Westerners had long thought Western education would sap the Moslem faith and added that the ulema strongly encouraged this idea with their continual cries of alarm. Then came the naturalization campaign, and who were the true Moslems—the religious leaders or the youth who worked to save Islam?

The ulema had been defeated on their own ground. Henceforth, it would be increasingly unlikely that the joint campaign for national liberation and modernization could be derailed by an Olympian thunderbolt from the "high priests."

The New Elite and the Idea of Mission

In conclusion, it may be useful to sketch some points of contrast between the generation that was to direct the fourth stage of Tunisia's development and that of the third stage.

The new elite of the final stage resembled neither the aristocratic Young Tunisians nor the conservative, urban-centered Old Destourians. Rather, it was largely made up of men of both modest and provincial origin, those who had most successfully mastered the techniques of modern, Western civilization by means of a modern, Western education. Although an elite, they remained identified with their origins, becoming the Tunisian "Populists." In the best log-cabin style, they vaunted their modest beginnings,[24] championed the cause of the "man in rags,"[25] the sharecropper, the urban worker, and the have-nots in general. The Old Destour's Le Libéral could criticize the French attempts to work with ignorant and docile "fellahs," while they avoided the "French-educated elite."[26] By contrast, however, the new elite identified itself with these masses and participated in demonstrations with the rank-and-file members. "The link sketched by our Bach Hamba," wrote Bahri Guiga, "has finally been established between the people and their intellectuals. The dream of all the young is to reinforce it more and more, while rejecting naturalization, the avowed object of which is to separate the men of the twentieth century from those of the second."[27]

The new elite had also found a working solution to the problem of modernizing without rejecting Tunisian society and culture. This was to combine intense patriotism with the idea of the intellectual elite's "mission," reinforced by a complete identification with the masses.

The long newspaper debate between Durel and Bourguiba in the late 1920's on whether Tunisian women should abandon the veil and Tunisian men the chechia served to clarify this idea of the new elite. It might seem surprising that Bourguiba, now the leader in the fight for modernization and female emancipation, ever defended the veil. But in the battle for national liberation, one could not lightly reject anything that identified

Tunisia and distinguished it from other countries. Durel was arguing against the veil from the standpoint of certain universal ideas about liberty and human dignity, to which Bourguiba retorted in the best tradition of Renan: "Thus the joys shared in common as well as the reverses and humiliations suffered in common—all of that still does not create, for M. Durel, between the children of this country any link, any sentiment of solidarity, any idea of the nation."[28]

But, of course, the new elite did want to move Tunisian society toward basically Western standards. To solve this dilemma, Bourguiba advanced a rather sophisticated idea of the elite's mission. He argued that it was necessary to give a society the time required to assimilate new ideas freely, without coercion, since the unity and cohesion of the social body must not be compromised. Good and evil are not absolutes. What might be excellent in Tunisia could be disastrous elsewhere. Bourguiba contended that he and his group were in the vanguard in insisting on reforms at Zitouna University much bolder than most students would dream of. "Thirty years ago such a stance would have been maladroit and would have unleashed in the Moslem world the same tempest of protests that are aroused today by the idea of breaking brutally with the veil and the *chechia.*" In short, "the role of the elite is not to force the pace to the point of completely detaching itself from the mass it is charged with guiding."[29] Many times, he concluded, this elite will have to take a step backward in order to re-establish contact with the masses, not to flatter them or keep them in servitude, but to guide them more surely and with better chance of success.

Perhaps the most important characteristic of this new elite— and certainly the compelling reason for its eventual triumph— was this new intensity of commitment. No longer was the elite to be simply a link and interlocutor between the indigenous society and the "superior" foreign culture. Nor was this new elite, like certain of the Old Destourians, merely fighting a limited battle according to well-defined ground rules. Rather, these men were committed to the leadership of Tunisian society until it was liberated from the dual bondage of its own backwardness and of foreign domination.

Their concept of leadership laid new stress on individual sacrifice and glorified martyrdom—an idea, like those of nationalism and patriotism, that was almost certainly of European inspiration. Its parallel with the European nineteenth-century Romantic movement—the concept of the hero, individual sacrifice for an ideal, the newly awakened interest in the common people as being somehow closer to nature, the belief that man can be the master of his fate—is too close to be dismissed. Of course, it is also true that in a few years, Habib Bourguiba was to be dubbed "Supreme Combatant," or as translated literally from Arabic, "the greatest of the fighters in the holy war." But there is no denying that this new emotional intensity represented a revolutionary move away from the medieval Islamic distrust of political power, acceptance of external restraints as divinely ordained and not to be resisted, and emphasis on the microcosm of individual and family. The abstraction that evoked strong feelings was not the state, nor even less the nation, but the whole Islamic community (*Dar al Islam*), and this Islamic community was deemed best served by each man living his own life in accordance with Islamic principles. The tension, the gnawing doubt, which might induce extreme behavior—good or bad—was almost lacking. "God wills for you the easy, He does not will for you the difficult."[30] "God does not charge any soul beyond its capacity."[31] Nor is it necessary that any man "bear the burden of another."[32]

The "something new" that this first generation of the Neo-Destour brought was "the feeling of the people that Habib Bourguiba and his colleagues were completely prepared to sacrifice and to accept dangers and punishment for the sake of their country."[33]

During the first imprisonment of the Neo-Destour leaders, the most striking expression of the new ideal of sacrifice came, as might be expected, from Habib Bourguiba. In November, 1934, while still in confinement at Bourdj-Leboeuf, he wrote in a letter he was able to smuggle out to Resident General Peyrouton:

I have always believed, following a proud maxim which still captivates me, that "it is not necessary to hope in order to act, nor to succeed in order to persevere." . . . [If you believe you have done only your duty] you will, I think, accord to me that I have done only what I believe to have been mine. Now duty has this peculiarity, that it brings its own reward and expects no remuneration from anyone. Thus, do not wait for either my submission or my remission, for then I would lose that which I value, the esteem of my adversary.[34]

This new sense of mission spearheaded the coming social revolution. Looking back, the next generation of Neo-Destour leadership could see more clearly the significance of the idea of sacrifice: "that the political battle without cannons or machine guns, provided it is led by tenacious men decided upon the supreme sacrifice and not troubled by the first defeats . . . will reveal an unconquerable moral force, which will end in breaking the morale of the adversary."[35] As a corollary of this idea, they could also boast: "To fatalists and partisans of *mektoub* he [Bourguiba] recalled by numerous citations from the Koran and by invoking the life of the Prophet that the Moslem religion is not one of asceticism and renouncement, and that in exalting the dignity of man and in holding him responsible for his acts [Islam] also places upon him the sacred duty of ameliorating his condition in this world. . . ."[36]

II. *The Era of the Neo-Destour*

CLEMENT HENRY MOORE

1. Modernization and the One-Party System

With the creation of the Neo-Destour in the early 1930's, Tunisia entered the last—and present—phase of its modernizing process. The new party led the Tunisian people not only in the fight for independence, but also to the realization of the modernist goals that the young Tunisians had first championed and that had been somewhat blurred under the leadership of the Old Destour. Once independence had been won, after more than two decades of struggle, the new party consolidated its power and embarked upon another, and still unfinished, task—the molding of a largely traditional society into a modern nation-state.

The single-party regime in Tunisia, as in a number of new countries, may be defined as one in which a mass party, having successfully fought foreign domination, exercises a virtual monopoly of political power under an inspirational leader. The case of the Neo-Destour suggests that such parties may be able to provide the political conditions needed for carrying out a modernist revolution even after their historic mission of decolonization is completed.

Single- or dominant-party systems are perhaps a necessary stage in the process of development. Wherever parliamentary democracy—and with it the competition of political forces—has been tried in young nations, it has proved painfully unadaptable and has generally led to a military takeover. Even Turkey, which has been represented as the prime example of successful modernization, did not escape the fate of other Asian nations that sought to imitate Western institutions before acquiring the conditions necessary for their eventual success. Elsewhere in the Middle East, the parliamentary system has reflected only the intrigues of small groups of men, power seekers who were unrepresentative and soon discredited. Where several parties have had mass support, as in Indonesia or Pakistan, their competition —in the absence of agreement on fundamentals—has led to bitter and fruitless struggle that invited the intervention of the military. The competition of parties seems relatively safe and constructive only when one of them holds a dominant position, as is the case in India. The formidable task of modernization seems to demand a marshaling of energies around a leader and a party—apparently the only practicable alternative is military dictatorship.

A political system geared to social and economic development must at the same time provide political stability and actively seek to transform the underlying society. In this difficult task, the political elite must share modernist attitudes and be able to agree upon concrete reforms. Furthermore, if the reforms are to meet an adequate response throughout the society, the elite must be able to communicate its purposes to the people and foster accord and a sense of dedication. Whether modernization is to be carried out as a gradualist or revolutionary process, the elite needs mass support and understanding. If this support is lacking, the elite's efforts are likely either to dissipate in a social vacuum, or to widen the gap, common to most transitional societies, between the modern and traditional sectors. The dual task of preserving the cohesion of the elite and the support of the masses seems to be the main role, and the main justification, of the single or dominant party. Its role is to elicit a degree of political cohesion that is indispensable to build and buttress a modern national community.

This process of nation-building, which usually lasts many years after independence, is the first and most vital element of the more general process of modernization. Although it is easy, before independence, to unite people through mass fervor and agitation, after independence a continued effort must be made to achieve durable nationhood. The nation requires not only a strong government, but institutions that can ensure the cohesion of the political elite and its communication with all sectors of the society, and that can harness nationalist fervor to the mundane but exacting tasks of development.

Whatever the constitutional form of government established by the single party, its virtual monopoly of political power suggests obvious dangers. However democratic his intentions, the party's inspirational leader may become a demagogue and, ultimately, a dictator. Unchallenged and complacent, the party may lose dedicated cadres and mass support and become the vehicle of a ruling clique. Or, faced with rising opposition, it may use increasingly authoritarian means to stay in power. If the single party is to obtain the full support of the people, it must make some effort to rule democratically.

What is involved here is not only the problem of human liberty, which many ambitious modernists would brush aside if incompatible with the demands of their revolution, but the problem of efficacy as well. For without political institutions and mores that give individuals and groups some freedom of expression, it is questionable whether the process of modernization can effect profound transformations in a society. The purpose of modernization is precisely to bring about both material advancement and opportunities for the self-realization of the individual. The latter not only provides the moral justification for the new political and social order, but is, to a large extent, the mainspring of its material success.

Nation-building—the creation of a politically cohesive society —thus involves more than emotional appeals to patriotic fervor, impressive ceremonies, the cult of the leader-hero, and the dedication of thousands of party militants. As Bourguiba himself has been fond of saying, the appeal to reason must complement the appeal to emotion. If the government is to be convincing, it must elicit the consent of the people through rational argument and the airing of grievances rather than through demagogy and the techniques of mass manipulation. If the regime is to form citizens rather than subjects, it must see that the masses receive an education in democracy through participation in decision-making, at least at the local level—this, in fact, may well be the most important test of the democratic character of the regime.

For democracy in the developing nations cannot be cast in the mold of the institutions functioning in the open societies of the West, if only because the single party precludes the competition of organized political forces, which to us, in the West, is the essence of democratic rule. New criteria must guide the student of politics in his search for the democratic aspects—actual and potential—of the one-party system.

2. The Political Background

By the time Tunisia achieved independence, in 1956, its nationalist movement had acquired three distinct advantages: unchallenged leadership, a well-organized party, and a long background of constructive conflict with the colonial power. Before exploring the new regime's methods of nation-building and evaluating its democratic aspects, it is useful to examine the historical advantages for their impact upon the single-party system.

Tunisia was fortunate in achieving independence at just about the right time—before too much blood was spilled but after it had acquired the makings of a political system. The substantial modernist elite that emerged as a result of the French impact upon the old society had had two decades in which to build a strong party and communicate its ideas to the society; it had achieved a consensus on goals and the unchallenged supremacy needed to carry out its revolution. During these decades Habib Bourguiba's tactics—his own sense of timing—helped to make the conflict with the colonial power constructive. Colonial domination, weakened by the worldwide depression of the 1930's and the ignominies of World War II, provided the common enemy against which the nation could be mobilized. But it also lasted long enough for the mobilized nation to seek independence, not as a final goal but as a beginning.

The long conflict with France was constructive because it challenged the nationalists to assimilate and adapt the democratic political culture of the French conquerors. During the 1920's and 1930's, liberal French schoolteachers molded the generation that was to lead the fight for liberation. Had the young elite been educated in postwar instead of prewar Paris, its commitment to democratic values might have been colored by admiration for international Communism and an excessive faith in rigid organization. Instead, the Neo-Destour militants absorbed the ideas and procedures of modern mass democracy.

The triumph of the Neo-Destour over its conservative rival, the Old Destour, as early as 1934, gave it time to seal the victory of modernism and Western ideas over pan-Arabism and other traditionalist causes. This was fortunate, for if the older party had been strong enough, it might have seriously embarrassed the Neo-Destour after independence, when the latter enacted the bold reforms necessary for modernization.

And it was perhaps the Communist takeover of the French CGT after World War II that decided the Socialist Resident General to recognize the General Union of Tunisian Workers (UGTT), which was of great assistance to the Neo-Destour Party before independence. The fact that the union was closely linked to the party made it easier after independence for the government to control workers' demands for the good of the nation.

Fortuitous timing, however, was not the only reason for Tunisia's successful modernization. Bourguiba and the Neo-Destour were the conscious and diligent agents of Tunisia's destiny. The conjunction of a leader-hero gifted as a tactician with an active and disciplined party was the mainspring of Tunisia's success.

The Leader

The son of a retired lieutenant in the Beylical Guard, Habib Bourguiba was born in 1903 at Monastir, one of the Sahel's most ancient cities. He was sent to study in Tunis at Sadiki College's elementary-school annex, then at Sadiki College and the Lycée Carnot. A schoolboy during the period of martial law in Tunisia (1912–21), he had childhood memories of the Djellaz riot and of the popular resentment toward Italians when they took over Libya in 1911.

Bourguiba joined the Destour Party in 1922, two years before he left for Paris to study law and political science on limited funds donated by an older brother. In Paris, he had many enthusiasms: French literature, psychology and pathology, the theater, even the Charleston. He also made many contacts with the French Left, becoming intimate with Dr. Materi, the one-time militant of the French Communist Party who was to become the first President of the Neo-Destour.

He returned in 1927, with his French wife and son, to practice law in Tunis. Looked down upon as a provincial by the old Tunis families, yet treated as an equal in French liberal circles, his ambiguous position perhaps encouraged his ambitious nature along a revolutionary path. Bourguiba claims that it was the Eucharistic Congress held in Carthage, with its aura of Christian crusading in Moslem Tunisia, that precipitated him into a career of nationalist agitation. He became an active contributor to nationalist newspapers, and in 1932, with the small circle of fellow university graduates who were to become the nucleus of the Neo-Destour Party, formed his own newspaper, *L'Action Tunisienne.*

Politics became a trial of will when, in September, 1934, Bourguiba and his friends were thrown into jail by the Protectorate authorities. He spent ten of the following twenty years in French prisons (1934–36, 1938–43, 1952–54). When he returned to nationalist activity in 1936, after his first imprisonment, he had already captured the imagination of the younger generation. During the two decades, he developed to a high degree the skills of the hero-statesman: an orator who could move his people in their own dialect, the organizer of an effective mass political organization, and the skilled negotiator and diplomat who could obtain independence for his country.

During these two decades, as the prime animator of the Neo-Destour Party, Bourguiba came to personify the new nation. As he justly said in 1959:

> It is rare that the events that make up the landmarks in the life of one man are integrated into the history of a people to such an extent that the man seems to incarnate his whole people. If this transposition has been brought about, it is because the man was able to be the sincere spokesman of the nation's conscience, and because he fought so much and so well for the people's cause that the movements in the lives of each came to merge.[1]

His unchallenged leadership provided not only continuity but also a set of political ideals and tactics that effectively shaped Tunisia's modernist ambitions. "Bourguibism," as it has been labeled by French journalists, is more properly a set of tactics than a political ideology. But while it is not a rigid doctrine, it does rest on Bourguiba's belief in democracy (in the radical tradition of Rousseau) and in the moral value of the individual. For Bourguiba, national sovereignty and independence are only a first step in the development of the Tunisian individual. To construct a nation is to mobilize each member of society, to convince him of the value of a national community in which he can achieve his aspirations more fully than under colonial domination—in short, to transform men into modern citizens.

Bourguibism has its social and economic aspect, for individual dignity is dependent upon social welfare and economic opportunity. During the depression of the 1930's, Bourguiba often appealed to the people not to pay taxes, and he sometimes defined sovereignty as the control of taxation by the people.*

But Bourguiba was too pragmatic to be the disciple of a theorist like Karl Marx. In 1931, he wrote: "Tunisia is a country of middle classes and peasants, those whom the radical represents in France and whom socialism is trying to capture by battering the brain of Karl Marx."[2] He rejected Marxism as a doctrine designed only for advanced industrial nations. Neo-Destourian socialism today can be better understood as an expression of socially oriented nationalism than as a variant of Marxism.

In order to realize Western ideals in a Moslem society, Bourguiba has developed a carefully articulated set of political tactics grounded in the Western philosophic tradition. He believes that it is rational persuasion—eliciting changes in individual attitudes—that underlies all lasting political, social, or economic transformations. Implicit in this belief is the assumption that one cannot really force a change, whether it be France's granting of

---

* For example, he told the olive-oil producers of the Sahel, when they complained about taxation, that the way to avoid being squeezed by the olive press was to join Bourguiba and grab the lever of the press.

independence to a weak Tunisia, or Tunisia's modernization in the face of the stubborn obstacles of tradition.

Bourguiba usually expressed confidence in the ultimate triumph—to the benefit of all concerned—of his "rational" proposals. But from the Romantics he also learned that appeals to the heart were sometimes necessary before the voice of reason might be heard. Echoing Bergson, he observed of the nationalist struggle:

> There was need for a driving force [*élan vital*]: a product of the heart and sentiment that would force men to endurance and action, create enthusiasm and maintain it in spite of the vicissitudes and failures of a long and unequal struggle. . . .
>
> On the other hand, there was the need for intelligence and reason to direct and channel this struggle toward our objective.
>
> . . . Both were necessary: the motive force and the steering helm.[3]

In Bourguiba the two components are linked: His energy—the actor and demagogue in him—provides the *élan vital*, while his aptitude for political calculation provides the "steering helm." He has little respect for political extremists; he once said of the pan-Arabs in Tunis and Cairo: "Their oriental mentality does not allow them to understand that politics is the art of attaining the possible."[4]

Bourguibism is best known as a style of political negotiation for transforming a colonial situation. It combines an intransigence upon principles with flexibility in the choice of means to implement them. Bourguiba once explained his tactics quite clearly:

> In the Middle East, Bourguibism has been interpreted to mean one thing only, and even that is misunderstood as "take what is offered and then ask for more." This is equivalent to saying that one should accept anything. As an illustration, the example is given of a debtor who, out of a debt of one hundred millimes, agrees to pay back one only. That is better than nothing, it is said, and the creditor has only to go on asking. No, that is not Bourguibism.
>
> In point of fact, Bourguibism accepts a partial compromise only insofar as it offers the possibility of taking everything that is owed.
>
> A better example could be taken from the art of strategy. Imagine that you are trying to take a fortress held by an enemy who is stronger

than yourself, and from whom you cannot take everything at one blow. If he offers to let you have, say, a path which is useless, there is no point in accepting the compromise. But if he abandons a strategic position capable of becoming a point from which the whole system of fortifications can be taken, it would be criminal to refuse. So long as I feel myself incapable of taking the whole citadel by force, I would be failing in my duty and harming the cause of my country if I refused to take a point which would enable me later on to take all the rest.[5]

When favorable compromises with France were not possible, Bourguiba switched to tactics of mass agitation. In 1938, he preferred to arouse the mobs against paying their taxes rather than continue negotiations with a weakened Popular Front government. In 1954, after two years in prison, Bourguiba decisively rejected the Voizard reforms, which called for a Tunisian parliament containing settler as well as indigenous representatives, because the implicit idea of Franco-Tunisian cosovereignty threatened future political advance. Instead, the Neo-Destour organized terrorism in the cities and launched a guerrilla uprising in the countryside. Bourguiba was willing to negotiate again only after Mendès-France promised internal autonomy. The crisis in the summer of 1961 over the French bases at Bizerte is only the most recent illustration of this carefully controlled use of intransigence and violence to obtain favorable compromises from France. Though here the tactics backfired, negotiation proved to be the lesser evil to harassed French governments.

While he led the fight for national sovereignty, Bourguiba was, at the same time, engaged in building a new Tunisian nation in accord with his concept of nationhood as a shared and living solidarity of popular sentiment. During the periods of tranquillity and compromise, with their concomitant of public liberties, Tunisians could be organized and educated as modern nationalists and party militants. During the periods of agitation, the masses could be inspired by the hero-leader to action and sacrifice for their country. The image of a shared struggle against colonialism struck a familiar Islamic chord. At the height of nationalist agitation in 1938, Bourguiba wrote: "It is really the march toward deliverance that is now going on. Every militant is convinced that he is participating in a grandiose epic, in a doubly sacred work for national liberation, both social and political."[6]

In independent Tunisia, the tactics of colonial liberation were applied to the task of developing the country. Underdevelopment replaced colonialism as the foe against which the nation was to be mobilized, and the masses were to support enthusiastically, as an act of patriotism, the strategy devised by Bourguiba and his planners.

The Party

Bourguibist tactics called for an efficient mass political organization. When favorable compromises with France were possible, Bourguiba needed a mechanism "to silence the demagogues and be obeyed and understood by the rank and file."[7] When he embarked upon a trial of force, he needed a mass army of nationalist demonstrators and sometimes an elite corps of terrorists. And if, underlying the tactics of nationalist assertion, the nation was conceived as a living solidarity based on shared purpose, the Neo-Destour was needed to organize the solidarity.*

On the day of its founding, March 2, 1934, the Neo-Destour already claimed a party apparatus of sorts. Created after a series of disputes between the majority of the Old Destour's Executive Committee and the activist minority of Bourguiba and his friends, the Neo-Destour was the product of a rump congress of dissident members of the older party. About sixty delegates, from forty-eight of the Destour's eighty local committees, attended the Congress, although Bourguiba's followers exercised unchallenged control over only a few of these local committees.

In defeating the Old Destour, the Neo-Destour triumphed over

* At a recent party congress Bourguiba revealed his formula for waging a successful independence campaign. Three basic assets must be assembled:

1. A minority of trained and dedicated shock troops supported by the active sympathy of the people.

2. Total confidence in the leader, entailing strict discipline of the militants and allowing the leader large room for maneuver with the assurance of always being understood and obeyed.

3. A well-planned strategy permitting intelligent use of the first two assets.

the old elite and thus ensured the victory of modernism. Taalbi's party revealed its weakness soon after his return to Tunisia in 1937, after fifteen years in exile. At first, efforts were made to reconcile the two Destours, and the new party tried to woo Taalbi as a figurehead. When this failed, the two parties entered into open competition for popular support. Because of its greater number of militants, superior organization, and rough tactics, the Neo-Destour succeeded in blocking Taalbi's speaking tours, and ridiculed him by forcing him to seek police protection against the very masses whose support he sought. Before he died, Taalbi testified in court against Bourguiba, who was on trial for his life for his role behind the bloody nationalist demonstrations of 1938. When the Neo-Destour published the testimony, Taalbi was utterly discredited. Although it survives today as a moribund party, the Old Destour was never again in a position to challenge the supremacy of its offshoot.

The Neo-Destour operated under severe handicaps. Before independence, it was never a parliamentary party, as the Protectorate did not foster institutions that included representative Tunisians. Moreover, it had to contend with colonial repression. In September, 1934, six months after it was founded, the party was legally dissolved, and it remained outlawed for the next twenty years. Even during Bourguiba's long dialogue with the Popular Front, from May, 1936, to April, 1938, the party had no legal existence, though its activities were tolerated. From 1938 to 1942, its leaders were all in prison and its activities were clandestine. During the German occupation of 1942–43, the Neo-Destour was allowed to reorganize, and following the Allied victory in 1943, the party, although again curtailed, continued to publish a newspaper. After 1948, the party was allowed to organize peaceful meetings and demonstrations. In January, 1952, with the arrest of its leaders, the Neo-Destour was again forced underground, and open political activity was tolerated only after Mendès-France's decision on July 31, 1954, to grant self-government to Tunisia.

The foundation for the Neo-Destour success as a nation-builder consisted in the quality of its leadership, its mass membership, its organization, and its use of other national organizations.

Guided by Bourguiba's brilliant strategy and tactics, the Neo-Destour made few political errors in its bid for power. In addition, Bourguiba had the good fortune to find and develop able political lieutenants who shared his modern activist approach to politics. Most of them had been educated at Sadiki College before going to France for their university work, and they comprised the cream of Tunisia's young modernist elite. United under the spell of Bourguiba's forceful personality, they helped him obtain the mass membership and run the organization needed to build the Neo-Destour into a dominant party.

The Neo-Destour rode the crest of a social revolution. The new party's main support came from the coastal towns and villages of the Sahel, where Bourguiba appealed primarily to the new middle classes rather than to the Old Destour's broad-based but entirely traditional elite. This difference helps to explain the success of the Neo-Destour, for socially and politically the newer classes, created but not compromised by the colonial situation, were more prepared to spearhead political change. It seems no accident that the village of Ksar-Hellal, situated in the center of the Sahel, midway between the cities of Sousse and Mahdia, was the site of the first Neo-Destour Congress. Having maintained its civilized, sedentary way of life even during the most disastrous Arab nomad invasions, the Sahel did not suffer the social and economic disequilibrium induced elsewhere by the settlement of the *colons*. Its traditions of village solidarity, coupled with the high concentration of population, prevented foreigners from buying land. With few exceptions, the only Europeans to come to the Sahel were schoolteachers and civil servants.

The widely distributed yeoman class of olive-tree cultivators living in Sahel villages made thrifty sacrifices to send their sons, ambitious and hardworking students on the whole, to modern secondary schools and French universities. This respect for learning also stimulated the development of private modern Koranic schools to spread primary education in the Sahel. Branded as outsiders (*afaqi*) in Tunis by the old Tunisois families (*baldi*), the young students from the Sahel banded together to widen their village solidarity into a regional solidarity that would be open to other *afaqi* and the poorer or more progressive natives of Tunis, thus providing a new core for national solidarity. Although some of the sons of the Tunis *baldi* joined the Neo-Destour, the majority of its leadership was *afaqi* and its most reliable shock troops were the country peasants and Tunis plebs.

Unlike the leaders of the Old Destour, who frankly confessed that they were interested in recruiting only the traditional intellectual elite, Bourguiba aimed squarely at the masses. As early as 1934, his young team was appealing to impoverished artisans and workers, peasants, and Bedouins, who throughout Tunisia's long history had never participated in the country's political processes. During the spring and summer of that year, the Neo-Destour leaders made constant trips from Tunis into the interior —an innovation in Tunisian politics—to set up new branches as well as to besiege the Old Destour committees. The ground was somewhat prepared for them by the severe drought of 1934–36, which intensified the sufferings caused by the depression.*

Crucial support for the Neo-Destour also came from the traditional artisans and merchants of the Tunis *souks*. They not only provided party funds, but a mass of sympathizers with a genuine grievance: They readily became nationalists because the colonial situation, by providing cheap imports from France, had impoverished them. By 1937, when the Neo-Destour was clearly outdistancing its older rival, they were rallying to the party.†

---

* Bourguiba took advantage of the desperate economic conditions to contact the camps where the authorities had regrouped the starving Bedouins. In this way he brought the Zlass tribesmen of the Kairouan area into the party. He could also count upon other tribes, like the Mouatiss, whom he had defended as a young lawyer in 1928. Though his tribal support in 1934 was neither widespread nor of great political significance, its very existence emphasized the image of the young party as a truly democratic organization interested in all Tunisians, however poor and ignorant.

† Significantly, Dr. Materi, son of an impoverished *baldi* family, was the first President of the Neo-Destour. Though less active than Bourguiba, he, rather than the hotheaded outsiders, could obtain the confidence of these traditional elements. Many became disaffected when Materi quietly resigned

From the outset of his political career Bourguiba naturally attracted the loyalties of most of the Moslem students of Sadiki College and the French *lycées,* with the exception only of some of the less impressionable sons of old Tunis families. He also appealed to many of the Zitouna students, although by training and temperament they belonged to a different world and indeed were jealous of the students at the more modern institutions. The sheiks of Zitouna either collaborated with the French authorities to attain official positions or turned to the revolutionary Taalbi, whose pan-Islamic outlook they shared. Despite the influence of their professors, many students were attracted by Bourguiba's dynamism. They were naturally a revolutionary group, coming from the disinherited classes of Tunisian society (even the sons of their professors often went to the better modern schools). Apart from small posts in the administration of Moslem justice, few jobs were open to graduates of Zitouna. Numbering 16,000 by independence, the students of Zitouna provided thousands of recruits for the Neo-Destour Youth.

The party's most reliable shock troops in Tunis, however, came from tribal groups that had emigrated from the south in search of employment. They generally formed tight communities, living and working together in Tunis. The Metouia, for instance, who came from a small oasis near Gabès, comprised the bulk of the Tunis longshoremen, and lived in a particular district of town. They had actively supported Mohammed Ali's trade union in 1924–25 and now formed one of the Neo-Destour's oldest and most militant branches.

The Neo-Destour was the first political organization to be truly open to Tunisians of all regions and classes. Statistics testify to the effectiveness of party recruitment over two decades. In July, 1954, while the party was still underground, it claimed more than 100,000 members. When later that year it was permitted to reorganize, the number grew to more than 325,000— or one out of every three adult male Tunisians.

The effectiveness of the party's organization had made this

---

in January, 1938, rather than endorse Bourguiba's increasingly intransigent tactics.

national mobilization possible. As one of the top Neo-Destour leaders wrote: "Trained in the Western school, they [the party leaders] borrowed from French political parties their tactics, their organization, and even their slogans."[8] Within three years of its founding, the Neo-Destour was carefully organized along the lines of parties of the French left. This structure served to discipline and politically educate the new members as well as to train cadres for both overt and clandestine political activity.

The formal structure, which changed little between 1937 and 1955, was both democratic and centralized. It was, in fact, modeled on the structure of the French Socialist Party. The party branches, or "cells" as they came to be called by the French-speaking populace, were located in almost every town and urban district and formed the base of the pyramid. Unlike the cells of Communist parties, they generally included hundreds of members and enjoyed contacts with one another. Their Executive Committees were freely elected at annual branch assemblies. The second echelon, the federations, supervised branch activities. Federation executives were also elected annually by the branch delegates to federal congresses. In 1937, there were more than 400 branches grouped in 17 federations, and by 1955 the party had 1,000 branches and 32 federations.

The National Congress, made up of delegates from all the branches, was the supreme authority of the party. The Congress elected the Political Bureau, the highest executive authority. It also chose roughly half the membership of the National Council, the other half being made up of one delegate from each of the federations. The National Council served as an interim body to supervise the work of the Political Bureau between meetings of the National Congress. The five- to ten-man Political Bureau, aided by appointed permanent commissions for youth, propaganda, economic affairs, and finances, gave directives to the federations, which were in turn transmitted to branches. This efficient chain of command was also democratic: The Political Bureau was responsible to the National Congress and to the National Council. The politically sophisticated federation leaders, too, exercised judgment and discretion in their overseeing of local party activities. Generally of modest, typically Zitouna education, they were the party's cultural as well as political link between the university-trained Political Bureau and the rank and file.

The practice of the party was, of course, somewhat different from its paper structure, for political conditions in Tunisia were always changing. Although the National Congress was supposed to meet annually, only two genuine Congresses were held in the twenty years before self-government. Generally, the National Council or even the Political Bureau replaced the National Congress as the forum in which political decisions were taken. And much of the time, when the leaders were under arrest, there was no forum. Then, an *ad hoc* structure took shape whereby the second-string leadership that had not been arrested exercised responsibility. Those federations that could remain active had wide latitude. By 1952, the party had acquired sufficient experience in clandestine organization to remain intact during two years of repression. Clandestine Political Bureaus succeeded one another and kept control of propaganda activities and terrorist rings—usually made up of Neo-Destour Youth who in more normal circumstances were responsible for keeping order at public rallies. As testimony to the effective organization of the party, the Political Bureau managed in 1954 largely to supply and to control the 3,000-man guerrilla "Army of Liberation."

The greatest accomplishment of the party apparatus was its ability to form cadres. The Neo-Destour Youth was the most important training ground, and by independence had about 100,000 members. The party not only used them as shock troops, but taught them the lessons of Bourguibism and prepared the more promising of them for responsibilities in the regular party apparatus. Thus many cadres—and some of the top leadership today—acquired at an early age a solid political education and loyalty to the national cause. The federations were another important training ground for politically sophisticated leaders, who by background and education remained close to the people.

The party's hold on its members after independence was due

primarily not to rigid doctrine but to the creation before independence of thousands of devoted activists. The militants were taught to take initiative, to question colonial authority, and to sacrifice themselves for the nation. The party became their second, and sometimes their only, home, as they led their country into the modern world.

An important reason for the success of the Neo-Destour in mobilizing the people in the struggle for independence lay in its relations with the so-called "national organizations." Before independence, the Union Générale des Travailleurs Tunisiens (UGTT) had approximately 100,000 members, and the Union Tunisienne des Artisans et Commerçants (UTAC), about 40,000. Two other important interest groups were the Union Générale des Agriculteurs Tunisiens (UGAT) and the Union Générale des Etudiants Tunisiens (UGET). Bourguiba has subsequently explained that these organizations were controlled by the party and were "tactically necessary, to keep some elements outside the party and protect them from repression and the risks of overt political activity."[9] Indeed, with the exception of the UGTT, the national organizations were founded on party directives by trusted militants who took all their orders from the Political Bureau.

The case of the UGTT, by far the most important of the national organizations, was somewhat different. Autonomous Tunisian trade-unionism, as distinguished from the settler-controlled section of the CGT, had traditions dating back to 1924, although attempts to organize a Tunisian union had failed both then and in 1938. The Bourguiba of Tunisian labor, Ferhat Hached, a veteran leader of the CGT in Sfax, founded the UGTT in 1946. Though he was not a member of the Neo-Destour, most of his top leadership came from the party.

Past failures indicated that a true Tunisian labor union could be successful only if it was tightly allied with the nationalist party to present a common front against colonial domination. Hached and his union, while working for immediate, limited, professional gains, considered national autonomy to be a necessary condition for achieving social justice. When the Neo-Destour was suppressed in 1952, the authorities did not dare outlaw the UGTT, which was closely allied with American labor through the International Confederation of Free Trade Unions. A sign of the two-way relationship between the party and the UGTT was Hached's leading place on the clandestine Political Bureau until his assassination by a European terrorist group in December, 1952.

In the ten years prior to independence, the UGTT developed into an effective representative of workers' interests and was to a certain extent respected as such by the colonial authorities. Though less effective, the other professional organizations also developed concrete grievances against the regime. Especially after 1952, when the Neo-Destour tried to internationalize its dispute with France, the UGTT's contacts abroad proved invaluable.

The party's relationship with the national organizations proved to be of long-range significance. Well-organized interest groups, usually lacking in new countries, were developed early in Tunisia. Thus, they were psychologically prepared by their activities in the struggle for independence to sacrifice their less essential interests for the sake of nation-building.

Although by the time of independence the party apparatus extended throughout the country, its strength was not uniform. It was weakest in the southern tribal areas under French military occupation. Some of the fertile areas of the North, where settler farms were concentrated, were also less politically developed— despite constant contact with the Europeans—than other areas like the Sahel, which had few settlers. Political organizing was difficult where the settlers, supported by the local authorities, had systematically suppressed the Neo-Destour. Although the UGTT reached some of the agricultural workers on settler farms, the Sahel tradition of village solidarity offered a much firmer foundation for nation-building. But two decades gave the party enough time to acquire solid roots in most regions.

Before independence, Tunisia had an asset shared by few

other new countries. The nationalists had created what amounted to a political system, outside the unrepresentative system of the Protectorate. The Neo-Destour and the national organizations were reflecting the *pays réel*—to use a French and Neo-Destourian expression—as opposed to the *pays légal*. The new system guaranteed national cohesion by fostering a tacit consensus. Tunisia's political background seemed ideally suited to produce a single-party regime that could serve both political requirements of modernization—the building of the new nation and the development of democratic institutions.

3. Nation-Building

The transfer of power from the colonial authority to the citizens of the new nation was to take a full five years—from the appointment by the French in 1954 of a Tunisian Government to negotiate the Conventions that would grant home rule to Tunisia to the proclamation, on June 1, 1959, of independent Tunisia's constitution.

Ahmed Ben Salah, today one of the most influential ministers in the Tunisian Government, reflected the constructive philosophy of the Neo-Destour when, after the first hurdles had been crossed, he wrote: "The process of decolonization should not be the opposite of that of colonization. This revolution is not the destruction of the fruits of colonization, but their utilization and fundamental reorientation."[1] In retrospect, the pattern of political decolonization in Tunisia seems to have been a miracle wholly justifying the methods of Bourguiba—a gradual, careful process carried out in an atmosphere that might readily have lent itself to extremist solutions.

The Conventions signed with France, after long and delicate negotiations, were such a compromise that only the prestige of Bourguiba could have persuaded the Neo-Destour to support them. The French had reserved for themselves the management of Tunisia's foreign affairs and defense; they would continue to control the modern sector of the economy and to hold many of the administrative posts. Especially rankling to the nationalists were the provisions whereby France would continue to control the internal security services and the police.

Bourguiba was well aware that the opposition to the Conventions voiced by the party's General Secretary, Salah Ben Youssef, would strike a sympathetic echo in Tunisian public opinion. He therefore sent his aides, Mongi Slim and Mohamed Masmoudi, both of whom had participated in the negotiations, on a tour of the country just before the signing of the Conventions to explain their provisions to Neo-Destour branches and to labor leaders. When Bourguiba returned to Tunisia on June 1, 1955, mammoth crowds gave his homecoming the character of a national plebiscite—not only for the man, but also for the Conventions upon which he had staked his political career. The Neo-Destour appeared to be a united party whose leaders had convinced the rank and file of the need to cooperate once again with France. During that summer, despite the hardships brought by a bad harvest, plans for the investiture of the new Tunisian Government proceeded smoothly. It seemed that a gradualist approach to decolonization could be taken, despite the continued opposition broadcast from Cairo by Salah Ben Youssef.

Preferring that Ben Youssef pursue his policy of opposition in Tunisia, Bourguiba persuaded him to return from exile, met him at the airport, and escorted him into Tunis in a lavish display of party unity. Whether because of jealousy of Bourguiba or true political differences deepened by his years in Egypt, Ben Youssef chose to ignore attempts at reconciliation in the name of party unity. Less than a month after his return, he blasted all hopes for unity by delivering a Friday sermon in the venerable Zitouna Mosque. Before a huge crowd, Ben Youssef denounced the Conventions as a sell-out to colonialism. He called for a Neo-Destour policy of complete independence and for a meeting of the National Congress of the party.

Ben Youssef was expelled from the party by the Political Bureau the following day. For the next two months, however, he claimed, as had Bourguiba and his clique in 1934, that he was the only true leader of the Destour. In reality he was attempting— with significant success—to woo old militants into a new rival structure. Bourguiba's efforts to maintain the cohesion of the party were hindered by the fact that party stalwarts could not be rewarded immediately with government jobs. In addition, many nonparty Tunisians, including court circles, the sheiks of the Zitouna, rich landlords, and other notables, hoped for sympathy from Ben Youssef if he came into power. His pan-Arab and pan-Islamic slogans imported from Cairo appealed to them. Born on the island of Djerba, he also had the almost automatic support of his compatriots, who form an important class of grocers and merchants throughout Tunisia. But his greatest support came from the least politically educated sectors of the population—backward tribes and the uprooted youth of the cities. "Youssefism" was more a frame of mind than an ideology; it closely reflected the extremist attitude of many unsettled Tunisians in search of an Islamic or Arab identity.

Bourguiba hoped to persuade Tunisians of the correctness of his policies, while allowing Ben Youssef the freedom to propound his own point of view. If the experiment had been successful, the paradox of attempting to establish a truly democratic constitutional state based upon a single party might have been resolved. But the "liberal" competition of rival parties was possible for only a few months. The Neo-Destour Congress, held in mid-November, 1955, endorsed Bourguiba's policies, and the turning point was reached. With Bourguiba's clear-cut victory in a forum that Ben Youssef refused to recognize or attend, Ben Youssef "declared war" on the government and resorted to terrorism and armed uprising. In January, 1956, he escaped a police net and fled to Tripoli; but it took until June, 1956, to pacify the remnants of his guerrilla army in the south.*

The history of Youssefism has had serious consequences for Tunisia. The general atmosphere of insecurity that it created reinforced authoritarian trends within the party and government. The chaos resulting from open disagreements on fundamental issues forced most Tunisians to conclude that national unity transcended all other goals. Thus, the prudent uniformity that has characterized political life since independence has rested largely upon bad memories of a virtual civil war. Tunisia's leaders seem to have been shocked by the irrational reactions of mobs that had theretofore been on their side. As one Neo-Destour

---

* Ben Youssef subsequently resided in Cairo. He was assassinated in Frankfurt on August 12, 1961. (At this writing, the crime remains officially unsolved.) He remained to his death a violent enemy of Bourguiba; as late as 1958, there was a Youssefist plot against Bourguiba's life.

leader commented, "If you put them in a bottle, they will take its shape."

The Transfer of Power

Although Bourguiba was severely threatened by Youssefism, he was aware of its usefulness as an argument for extracting further concessions from the French. With France's granting of independence to Morocco on March 2, 1956, he was able to convince Guy Mollet, the Prime Minister of France, that Tunisia, too, merited absolute independence. The independence Protocol was signed on March 20, 1956.

The Protocol, however, granted only formal independence pending revision of the Conventions. Although most of the rights of an independent country were quickly obtained—including control over the police and foreign affairs and the beginnings of an army—areas of disagreement with France remained for years.

"Tunisification," the substitution of Tunisian for French administrative personnel, proceeded rapidly after independence, largely because of the number of educated Tunisians and seasoned party militants available. By 1957, few of the original 13,500 French civil servants remained in Tunisia. Nearly 1,000 French schoolteachers—many of them new recruits—were working for the Tunisian Ministry of Education, and about 1,600 other French civil servants were scattered throughout various branches of the administration. Reliable elements of the party youth and scouting organizations provided most of the personnel for the 2,000-man urban and 3,000-man rural police.

The leadership of the Neo-Destour was sufficiently broad-minded to recruit or keep capable nonparty men in the civil service, although loyal party members got the best jobs. The administrative structure of the Protectorate was kept virtually intact since it was staffed by Tunisians who had assimilated French administrative techniques. Thus a certain rigidity and lack of delegation of authority has remained in the system, with one or two notable exceptions. The administration has been criticized as being top-heavy and too ambitious for a poor country. Yet it is relatively efficient and has been remarkably free from corruption.*

Unlike many other newly independent countries, Tunisia has not created a conspicuous "new class" of government officials, although Tunisian have-nots sometimes express the opposite opinion. High government officials may receive as little as $4,000 a year, and a university graduate will be lucky to make half that much at the start of his government career. Although official cars and easy credit for housing accompany many government jobs, the administrators do not appear to be getting rich. A spirit of self-sacrifice and a willingness to learn seem to characterize the new Tunisian administration. These qualities, admirably reflecting Bourguibism, provide an ethos necessary to a country in the process of development.

Despite continued Youssefist disorders in the south, the first step of the new government after independence was to hold general elections for a Constituent Assembly. Elections were held on March 25, 1956. Although the Tunisian Communist Party protested the straight majority list voting (rather than proportional representation), it freely participated with lists in twelve of the eighteen constituencies. The Neo-Destour swept the elections with its National Front lists. In an important sense the elections were predetermined, for the candidates who won had been nominated by the party in consultation with the national organizations. Of the ninety-eight deputies, ten were unaffiliated notables whom the party had selected in the interests of national unity, and about twice that number had risen in the ranks of the trade union. Yet the Neo-Destour list was representative of political forces in the country, even though it was drawn up privately by Bourguiba and his lieutenants.

In the spring of 1957, elections were organized for ninety-four town councils, thirty of which were newly created. The freely elected councils were to build the foundations of democracy in

---

* Tunisian standards can be measured by the fate of a former high official recently convicted for corrupt practices. He was sentenced to ten years of forced labor for having made irregular allowance loans of a few hundred dollars to some of his colleagues, and for having bribed an insurance agent to insure his car after it had been in an accident.

Tunisia by encouraging local responsibility. For the first time, women were allowed to vote. Subsequent elections for the new National Assembly, in 1959, and for the town councils, in 1960 and 1963, have provided all Tunisian adults further opportunity to participate in the political process. Since 1960, the party has had no opposition; its only problem at election time has been to ensure that as many men and women as possible voted.

It was originally hoped that the status of the independent Tunisian Government would be rapidly regularized by a new constitution. But, in fact, the Constituent Assembly sporadically deliberated constitutional proposals for more than three years. During the summer of 1956, when Bourguiba launched important social reforms, the Assembly, which had barely begun its work, was not consulted. But the political events of the following year help to explain why constitution-making was such a slow process.

In a ceremony on July 25, 1957, carefully prepared by the Neo-Destour, the Constituent Assembly deposed the bey—Tunisia's hereditary absolute monarch through whom the French had ruled—and proclaimed Tunisia a republic. It also provisionally named Bourguiba President of the Republic and, giving him the executive and legislative powers only formally possessed by the bey, established the precedent for the Presidential regime that it would subsequently make constitutional. Bourguiba replaced the bey's council of ministers with a Cabinet responsible only to himself, and limited the role of the Constituent Assembly, apart from drafting a constitution, to one of consultation at the will of Bourguiba's government.

Two years later, on June 1, 1959, the new constitution went into effect. The government it established was patterned upon the American Presidential system, with traces of the French Fifth Republic. The President, who is elected for a five-year term and must be a Moslem, has more power than either the American President or the British Prime Minister. He makes policy and selects a Cabinet responsible only to him. He has priority in sponsoring bills. He has the right to veto legislation, although he can be overruled by two-thirds of the National Assembly. He can address the Assembly at will. The deputies to the Assembly are not allowed to set up investigation committees, and in practice they meet in plenary sessions only to adopt Bourguiba's legislation. The President may, and often does, sidestep the Assembly by issuing decree laws during the six months of the year when it is not in session. In times of "danger threatening the safety and independence of the Republic," the President may take "exceptional measures" about which he informs the Assembly.

With the exercise of power successfully transferred into Tunisian hands and regularized by the principles of constitutional democracy, the twenty-five-year dream of Bourguiba and his party had become a reality. The continued legal existence of two opposition parties, the Old Destour and the Communist Party, suggested that the Neo-Destour was sufficiently open and tolerant in its hour of victory to try to encourage the nascent democracy that, largely unaided, it had established. The open personality of Bourguiba was another encouraging factor. Time and again since independence he had fought privately and in public speeches against the tendency of party militants to arrogate undue privileges as the spoils of victory.

But nation-building remained a precarious process as long as revolutionary war raged in nearby Algeria. Naturally, France desired to maintain French troops on Tunisian soil, if only to prevent Algerian rebels from using Tunisia as a base or haven. Even when the Tunisian frontiers were evacuated, France continually evoked the "right of pursuit," finally bombing the Tunisian border village of Sakiet-sidi-Youssef early in 1958. One of the first moves of General de Gaulle, when he came to power in the spring of 1958, was to agree on the evacuation of all French forces in Tunisia to the base of Bizerte, with the understanding that the status of the Bizerte base would be negotiated later. But no agreement was reached on Bizerte until July, 1962, one year after the bloody four-day battle that cost more than 1,300 Tunisian lives.*

* Bizerte seems to have been a tragic misunderstanding. Bourguiba apparently aimed at a political rather than a military action. In addition to regular troops and the National Guard, his "army" at Bizerte included Scouts, women, the Neo-Destour Youth, and truckloads of unemployed. Bourguiba probably miscalculated the French reaction, which was brutal and

Other lingering bones of contention were the fate of more than a million acres of rich *colon* real estate and the definition of the Saharan frontiers. Tunisian cohesion after independence was perhaps tightened by these long-standing grievances against the former colonial power. But when taken together with the Algerian problem, which underlay all of Tunisia's relations with France, it can be seen that the little country required skilled leadership to survive at all. The Algerian War placed Bourguiba on a diplomatic tightrope: In order to build his nation, he had to be careful to do nothing that would cause the generalization of the conflict, which a segment of French opinion wanted; on the other hand, he had to give tangible support to the nationalist movement of a brother people who would one day be a powerful neighbor.

Tunisia's support of the Algerians meant the loss, only one year after independence, of $50 million a year in French economic aid. It also meant housing a large exiled Algerian army, tens of thousands of Algerian refugees, and the Provisional Algerian Government. All this was done without precipitating a serious crisis with France, but these seven tense years required deep national cohesion in support of a demanding, but unglamorous, foreign policy.

The new regime was able to embark upon a spectacular series of social reforms, but in the delicate diplomatic context, the time was not ripe for drastic economic reforms, such as the sweeping nationalization and economic planning advocated by the powerful UGTT. Such demands had to be stifled during the drive to consolidate the new regime. But once his power was secured, in late 1959, Bourguiba launched the second phase, the "battle against underdevelopment." He finally picked up the old ideas of the trade union, labeling them "Neo-Destour socialism," and placed their exponent, Ahmed Ben Salah, in charge of economic

---

effective. He also miscalculated the long-term consequences of his move: Many French and Italian settlers left the country in panic, despite the circumspect handling of foreign residents by the Tunisian authorities. An important by-product of the affair was the difficulty in recruiting enough teachers for the school year 1961–62.

planning; by 1961, with the publication of a Ten-Year Plan, Tunisia's experiment of planned social and economic development had begun.

PRESERVING NATIONAL UNITY

The Role of the Leader

Together with the creation of new institutions, the main task of both leader and party was to build and maintain national cohesion.

Habib Bourguiba has been a sovereign who rules as well as reigns. He has quasi-absolute power as head of state and as head of the party, and his sense of mission and powerful personality prod him into making full use of his extensive constitutional power. Taking into account Bourguiba's tendency to dramatics, this statement by him in defense of his powerful role is probably quite accurate:

> The fact that I now have more authority than I had before is for the good of this people. I listen to advice, I discuss, I change when I am mistaken, for like everyone, I can make mistakes and do not feel immune from error. I remain open to all confrontations. Aside from the respect due to my position and my past, I enjoy the affection of the men about me. This is a considerable privilege.[2]

The pageantry surrounding Bourguiba wherever he goes undoubtedly impresses the masses more than it does the educated elite. In fact, in his taste for ostentatious display, he sometimes gives the impression of acting a part for their benefit in order to inculcate the habit of respect for the state that he embodies. Traditional respect for the monarchy, transferred to his person, thus possibly serves as a focus for national cohesion.

As the undisputed ruler, Bourguiba has retained and developed his role as the educator of his society. Over the heads of the deputies and party officials, he maintains constant contact with the people by all the media of modern communications. He travels regularly in the countryside as though constantly contesting an election, using his many speaking occasions to try to instill in the people a sense of their dignity as individuals and citizens. As the self-styled father of his people, he gives advice on such matters as personal tidiness and cleanliness, decent housing, the importance of sports, the desirability of sedentary village life. As the ruler of a Moslem country, he claims the right to reinterpret Islam, emphasizing that true Islam liberates the individual by encouraging him to use his intelligence.

Bourguiba is not worshiped as a holy man, a *marabout*. Neither he nor his audience believes that he possesses some mystic inner quality. The man's great popularity, however, seems in some measure a reflection of this Tunisian tradition. People flock to see him, to hear his voice, to feel his presence—whether or not they listen to what he says. Had he lived in another age he might have been an acclaimed leader of a religious order.

One of Bourguiba's greatest talents as a politician is not seen by the public, but is corroborated by leading Tunisian officials. This is a behind-the-scenes talent "to cooperate with others and make them cooperate with each other and with him."[3]

He personally makes all key appointments in both the party and the government, a power which he has used with great skill. Though he takes advice about appointments from both his official subordinates and private advisers, he tolerates no criticism once he has chosen his man. He also shuffles the members of his Cabinet about, perhaps to make sure that they do not become entrenched in their domain. Only two of the ministers of the original 1956 Cabinet remained in 1962.[*]

A tempering quality of his great power is Bourguiba's willingness to hear good arguments—in private—in criticism of his policies. Frank and straightforward himself, he likes this quality

---

[*] Cabinet members often hold key posts in the party as well as in the government. Bahi Ladgham, who replaced Salah Ben Youssef as General Secretary of the Neo-Destour, is also Minister of Defense. Taieb Mehiri is second to Ladgham in the party as well as Minister of the Interior. Mongi Slim, who was in charge of the party apparatus during the 1940's, preceded Mehiri as Minister of the Interior during the period of the Conventions. He was then sent as Tunisia's ambassador to Washington and the United Nations. He returned to Tunisia in 1962 to serve as Minister of Foreign Affairs.

in his subordinates and is often disappointed by their servility. He also constantly consults, especially with the members of his Cabinet and the Political Bureau, before making any important policy decision. Thus his ideas have sometimes developed under the impact of people as well as of circumstances.

Another quality of Bourguiba is his willingness to forgive. Except for Salah Ben Youssef, with whom reconciliation was impossible, and for a few of Ben Youssef's hired killers, who were hanged, the hundreds of imprisoned Youssefists were pardoned long before serving their time. Some of them were even appointed to key official positions. In 1962, a popular trade-unionist, sentenced as a Youssefist in 1958 to twenty years of forced labor, walked out of prison into a position on the board of directors of Tunisia's new quasi-governmental steel company. In 1961, Bourguiba placed a Youssefist ex-leader of the UGAT in charge of the State Domains Office to help carry out land reforms under the new Ten-Year Plan. Such tactics have helped to keep most of the capable members of the political elite within the system.

Although this elite is relatively homogeneous in outlook, a split within the Neo-Destour has always been a possibility. Ben Youssef might have formed a conservative opposition party based on pan-Arab sentiment in Tunisia. The UGTT might have become a labor party under its ambitious leader, Ahmed Ben Salah. The liberals in the Neo-Destour, with the support of students and those younger university graduates who had been left out of top positions, might have rebelled against single-party rule.

The explanation for political unity is more than Bourguiba's overpowering personality, his ability to inspire loyalty and to balance off his associates—the dynamic framework of the Neo-Destour Party is also important. It has provided not only a training ground but a forum for discussing political alternatives. After the Youssefist fiasco, any move to create a rival organization was considered too risky. With this knowledge, the two *enfants terribles* of postindependence politics, Ben Salah and Mohamed Masmoudi, never attempted a frontal assault on the party, however much Bourguiba strained their loyalties to him. They had no alternative but to retire or to submit to President Bourguiba.

The case of Ahmed Ben Salah may well be the best illustration of Bourguiba's tactics for maintaining cohesion in his party and his country. Barely thirty years old, Ben Salah in 1956 was at the crest of his popularity. As leader of the powerful UGTT he was getting almost as many headlines as Bourguiba. After being offered a minor ministry in Bourguiba's first government, which he refused, he began calling for the renovation of the doctrineless Neo-Destour through fusion with the UGTT. He demanded that the party adopt his radical economic program, although Bourguiba had already proclaimed policies protecting private foreign investments. To curb Ben Salah, Bourguiba encouraged a scission within the workers' union. The new union, created by Habib Achour, a veteran trade-unionist jealous of the university-educated Ben Salah, called for the development of a professional trade-unionism completely divorced from politics and the resignation of Ben Salah as the preconditions of reunification of the labor movement. Ben Salah was forced to resign as General Secretary of the UGTT in December, 1956. He was replaced by Ahmed Tlili, a member of the Political Bureau and Treasurer of the Neo-Destour as well as a veteran trade-unionist.

Bourguiba castigated Ben Salah, saying: "We must avoid generating resentment, sowing seeds of division under cover of foreign doctrines and principles that we would be ill-advised to want to apply to our country." Recalling that national unity was actually strengthened after the departure of Salah Ben Youssef, Bourguiba continued:

> The same goes for trade-union unity. It has been compromised these last weeks; leaders of the labor movement have found themselves in the logical necessity of getting rid of elements which, within the world of labor, were at the origin of the difficulty. To block the road to erroneous orientation, the leaders of the labor movement themselves have had to take measures necessary to preserve the interests of workers and to reattain trade-union unity, which will soon flower anew, I hope, in the framework of national unity.[4]

A few months later, Ben Salah emerged from retirement to be appointed Minister of Public Health, a post in which he could do no harm and in which his ambitions could serve the regime. He was named Minister of Plan and Finance in January, 1961. In four years, Bourguiba had turned a political adversary into a right-hand man.

Another occasional opponent, Mohamed Masmoudi, was first brought to heel in September, 1958, when the weekly newspaper under his patronage, *L'Action,* proved too critical as the organ of the liberal conscience of the party. Charging it with an "insidious campaign of confusion," the Political Bureau withdrew its support from the paper, which promptly folded, and dismissed Masmoudi from his place on the Political Bureau for "serious lack of discipline." Returned to grace a few months later as Minister of Information, Masmoudi was again removed from his office in November, 1961, after criticizing *"pouvoir personnel,"* the "cult of personality," in an editorial in *L'Action's* successor, *Afrique-Action.* Ironically, Ben Salah was appointed to the Political Bureau the very day that his long-standing rival, Masmoudi, was dismissed.

The Role of the Party

Bourguiba's skill as a politician is matched by his able handling of a powerful political machine. He has remained President of the Neo-Destour after independence, although Bahi Ladgham and Taieb Mehiri are the men most involved in its day-to-day operations. No organizer, Bourguiba knows enough to leave this part of running the party to others. He uses the party to keep in close touch with its ranking cadres and as an instrument to maintain contact with the masses. Ladgham and Mehiri have to answer the sometimes embarrassing questions of the militants at party congresses, while Bourguiba usually manages, as with the National Assembly, to remain above the debate. In a time of real crisis, however, Bourguiba knows how to take control. When the 1955 National Congress of the Neo-Destour dallied and hesitated, hoping for the impossible—a compromise between Ben Youssef and himself—Bourguiba took the floor and with a blistering burst of argument and eloquence forced the almost unanimous passage of a resolution that he had personally drafted.

Just as Bourguiba needed the party as organized support for his tactics of national liberation, he continues to need it to build his regime. The new state, however, has taken precedence over the party. Although the Neo-Destour provided the state with administrators, the party was not to govern but rather to support the government. Even the policy-making function of the Political Bureau was minimized. The entire party apparatus had to be transformed into an efficient but docile instrument of the state.

The process of transformation was not easy. By late 1957, the problem of the relationship between party and government had become acute. Bourguiba insisted that the state must be reinforced by harmonizing its structures. "Each wheel cannot turn on its own, independent of the others. . . . The state has the right to demand of its servants integrity, competence, and coordination of efforts."[5]

Hastily appointed militants were proving incompetent in their new government jobs or were caught misusing their positions to further the personal interests of friends in the party. Patronage demands were paralyzing the government apparatus. In the provinces, the problem was making long-standing local rivalries even worse. Old militants, regardless of their capacities, felt that they had the right to lucrative positions as a reward for past sacrifices. The party at the local level did not always respect even the rule of the powerful governors. Having placed themselves above the law for so many years, old militants found it hard to suddenly respect it.

To complicate matters, the party was swamped with new recruits—600,000 members were claimed in 1957—while the experienced cadres were lost to government service. Many of the educated new arrivals did not take to party discipline, and older members were disdainful of those who had waited to join the winning team. For many, party membership was a steppingstone to a career in the civil service or a way of expressing loyalty to Bourguiba. For many others it was simply a means of finding a job or a place for their children in school.

In October, 1958, Bourguiba announced his long-expected reform of the party apparatus. The federations, whose officers had been elected by the branch leaders, were replaced by regional offices, 1 in each of Tunisia's 14 governorates, headed by a commissioner appointed by the Political Bureau. The party's 1,800 branches were reduced to 1,000, 1 for each *sheikhat*. Thus the structure of the party would parallel the state's regional and local administration and be under the tight control of the Political Bureau.

In a long speech, Bourguiba tried to justify the structural changes in the party. He claimed that the federations were no longer necessary as centers of initiative, now that the Political Bureau was not endangered by colonial repression. Stressing the need for a strong centralized power, he explained:

> We need cohesion and discipline to increase efficiency. . . . It is indispensable that the party adapt its organization to the administrative armature of the country, so that the two structures support one another and progress in perfect harmony. . . . The reform in reality is not doing anything more than reducing the evils of the inflation of cadres. Some leaders, especially those who claim a glorious past of struggles and sacrifice, have paralyzed the activities of the administration by their constant interventions. . . . We cannot permit anyone to paralyze the state apparatus. Those who, by lack of consideration, are tempted to do so will be treated as enemies. . . . I will never be able to compromise, for whatever motive, on the necessity of ensuring the reputation of the state and its prestige.[6]

Six months later, shortly before the first serious clash between a governor and a party commissioner, Bourguiba tried to define their respective roles:

> There must exist a harmony in their action, so that, on the one hand, the governor, the executive agent of the government, does not undertake projects that the citizens have not been prepared to understand, and on the other hand, the commissioner, informed of these projects, works to prepare the ground.

He concluded with the decisive argument for harmony: "The governor and the commissioner are an emanation of my person."[7]

Serious conflicts seem to have been kept to a minimum. This is partly because governors and commissioners were often shifted.

Generally, too, the governors and commissioners had been militants together in the party and were able to cooperate on this basis. In the few cases of serious disagreement, the problem was forwarded to Bourguiba. Above all, there was remarkably little corruption under the new system.

Just as the party had to be made into a servant of the state, the special-interest organizations—all, with the exception of the UGTT, created by the Neo-Destour as instruments of the party's independence campaign—had to be retailored in the name of national cohesion.

The history of the UGTT scission is an example of the limited role of the national organizations in independent Tunisia. Ben Salah, the leader of the UGTT, wanted the union to continue to play a political role. Whatever structural links were devised between party and union, his organization should continue to serve as the instrument of social revolution. But the position of the government, as represented by Habib Achour, triumphed, and the UGTT was limited to the pursuit of workers' interests. In practice, the union has continued to take stands on issues of national policy, but these stands support government decisions. The apoliticization of the union was carried out to the extent that those unionists highly placed in the government had to resign from their union responsibilities. The close cooperation of union and party was assured by the positions of the new union leaders, Tlili and Achour, on the Political Bureau.

The farmers' union (UGAT) was realigned even before the UGTT when, in 1955, its leadership made the mistake of backing Ben Youssef in his bid for power. The Bourguibist press accused the union of being under the leadership of large landowners who were looking out for their own interests. A group from the Sahel broke away from the parent union, held a rump congress, which Bourguiba attended, and formed a new farmers' union, the Union Nationale des Agriculteurs Tunisiens. The old union was dissolved by governmental decree a few weeks later, and the new union took over its offices.

In 1960, the artisans' and tradesmen's union (UTAC) was renamed the Union Tunisienne de l'Industrie et du Commerce (UTIC), thus promoting artisans to the ranks of modern industry. When Bourguiba decided that economic planning was in the national interest, tightened control of this union became necessary. In 1962, the elected regional councils of the organization were replaced by economic committees appointed by the union's General Secretary, who is a member of the party's Political Bureau.

In 1963, it seemed that the national organizations would be even further integrated into the party apparatus: Just as the national leaders of UTIC and the UGTT were members of the Political Bureau, regional leaders would henceforth participate in new regional committees of the party. Moreover, the Neo-Destour was accelerating the formation of workers' branches in the cities. Despite the dissatisfaction of UGTT leaders, who wished their organization to remain autonomous, Tlili was encouraging the UGTT rank and file to join and take control of the new branches.

The students' organization (UGET) is the most nonconformist of the national organizations. Its members consider themselves "intellectual workers" whose interests, like those of other workers, must be defended. The union also considers itself to have a general political role as the representative of Tunisia's future elite. It has continued after independence to take positions on a whole range of political issues. Professing to be radical and progressive, it has advocated such policies as neutralism, recognition of Communist China, rigorous economic planning, limitation of private property, formation of agricultural producer cooperatives in place of private holdings, nationalization of all key industries, and rapid economic decolonization. Its leftist bent has been encouraged by the influence of some left-wing French professors in Tunisian schools, and by the fact that many Tunisians study in Paris.

With the help of a separate Neo-Destour student organization, however, the Neo-Destour manages to control the students somewhat, even though it cannot ensure that all of them always follow party discipline. The party's most effective lever of control has been the ambition of successive student leaders who have used their union as a springboard to a political career.

Within the context of the party's control, the special-interest organizations are allowed some play as pressure groups in the political process. Their officers are often elected to the National Assembly. They are also consulted by government departments on relevant legislation before it is sent to the Assembly. This behind-the-scenes process of reconciling diverse interests is well exemplified by the passage of a law on December 14, 1960, to reorganize social security.

In May, 1958, Ahmed Ben Salah, then Minister of Public Health and Social Affairs, wished to extend social security benefits to include all wage workers, notably those engaged in agriculture. The UGTT had long urged such a reform. In early 1959, Ben Salah presented draft proposals to the Cabinet and pushed his idea, revolutionary for a country accustomed to French social legislation, of limiting family allowances to cover a maximum of four children.

After two months of drafting sessions at the Presidency in the summer of 1959, the bill was forwarded to the UGTT, the UTIC, the Chambers of Commerce, European business directors, and doctors. Then for more than a year the draft legislation was stalled. Two Cabinet council meetings were held after an initial objection on the part of the UGTT; eventually Tlili, the union's head, received a guarantee that existing benefits would be maintained for families already having more than four children. At the Cabinet council of October, 1960, the draft law was formally approved. But before it reached the Assembly, UGTT representatives and an expert from Ben Salah's ministry agreed to a number of minor changes. Then, in an Assembly committee, the points of view of workers and employers were again brought forward through their deputies, and Ben Salah was questioned for five hours. The bill was finally approved in committee and was quickly ratified by the Assembly.

In a sense, the law's passage was a success for the UGTT over the UTIC, for the latter considered Tunisia unable to afford the luxury of extensive social legislation. Despite the flexibility of the law, it hurt many of the small shopkeepers and artisans who formed the bulk of UTIC's membership. On the other hand, the final bill represented an acceptable compromise. UTIC leaders recognized that its terms were favorable to the industries most important to Tunisia's growth. In over-all benefits, most workers made significant gains, while the rise in wages, not going into their pockets, did not threaten inflation.

The framing and passing of the social security bill typifies the process of consultation and compromise that characterizes Bourguiba's rule. Most of the discussion was not public. The newspapers reported only the final decision of the Cabinet council, together with interviews with Ben Salah and Tlili, and the National Assembly "debate," where the prearranged decision was simply ratified. The decisive push for the law came from Bourguiba. His numerous personal contacts, especially with Tlili and Ben Salah, were probably more significant than the official channels discussed above. The UGTT must have made it amply clear to Bourguiba that the workers, with salaries blocked or reduced since 1954, were in need of some major victory like the social security bill. In June, 1960, UTIC had secured its victory—the reorganization of arbitration boards and the passage of a law facilitating the dismissal of incompetent workers. Bourguiba thus seems to have carefully balanced the demands of workers and employers. When once he had decided upon the general principles of the new legislation, the national organizations were allowed to participate in its detailed elaboration.

The single-party regime thus allows in modest measure for the articulation of professional interests through the national organizations; these interests are balanced and effectively subordinated to the national interest by virtue of the party's control of the organization.

Mobilization of the Masses

In addition to being an arm of Bourguiba in the building of the nation, the Neo-Destour also serves to mobilize the masses in support of the regime and specific government projects. Even when elections are not in the offing, the party continues to act as if it were waging an electoral campaign. Whenever Bourguiba visits an area, the party erects triumphal arches in his honor and offers animal sacrifices. The masses, marshaled by squads of Neo-Destour Youth, are waiting to cheer Bourguiba hours before he arrives. At party meetings, it is normal procedure to send a telegram of support to the President of the Republic. Tunisia's many national holidays, anniversaries of important events in the nationalist struggle, are also occasions for the party to drum up patriotic fervor at mass meetings.

In times of crisis, the party is the defender of the regime and rallies the masses to its support. After the bombing of Sakiet, in 1958, the party not only kept perfect discipline but helped to man the barricades blockading French troops. In 1961, similar tactics proved disastrous at Bizerte, where the French forces killed or wounded 3,000 of the 10,000 poorly trained Neo-Destour Youth sent by the party to help the Tunisian Army blockade the French installations. On the other hand, the party rallied the masses after the disaster, and at hundreds of daily meetings in every corner of the country explained the fast-moving political developments to the people.

Apart from urging national solidarity, the party assists the administration on specific projects. It organizes annual health and sanitation campaigns and has most Tunisians busily planting trees on the annual Tree Day. It also organizes fund-raising drives for Tunisia's economic development, with the cooperation of the special interest organizations. To stimulate awareness of Tunisia's economic problems, the party branches were called upon in 1959 to devise, finance, and carry out local projects. Some created agricultural or industrial cooperatives, while most branches built classrooms or medical dispensaries. Since 1960, the party has placed "animators" on the government worksites for the unemployed, to encourage the 200,000 workers to feel that they are contributing to the "battle against underdevelopment," as well as to resolve any technical or administrative bottlenecks.

In Tunis and its suburbs, the party's branches have played a key role in the government's slum clearance program. They had to persuade tens of thousands of miserable, jobless Bedouins, who had flocked to shanty towns near Tunis before independence, to return to their native provinces where jobs would be made available. They also had to persuade more favored immigrants, sometimes in the dead of winter, to leave their mud huts to the demolition squads and await new housing. In the autumn of 1960, the party helped the State Domains Office to harvest the lands of settlers who had fled during the Bizerte crisis.

More generally, the party served the government by helping, in 1961, to create popular support of a planned economy. At Ben Salah's suggestion, the party organized a Week of the Plan, in June, when members of the Political Bureau lectured the party cadres and answered questions about the country's new economic orientation. In September, the party commissioners assembled committees in each governorate to discuss and report upon various aspects of the Ten-Year Plan. The reports were then distributed to the branches for comment and discussion. After this groundwork, the party formally committed itself in March, 1962, to backing the Plan at a four-day meeting of the National Council.

In its efforts to build a new society, the regime has been concerned less with mobilizing the masses than with attracting and educating the youth. Various organizations under party control exist for this purpose, the most important being the Neo-Destour Youth, the Scouts, and the students' union. Since independence the Neo-Destour Youth has suffered a steady decline, because it can no longer offer either the excitement of political agitation or—as local youth leaders constantly lament at branch meetings— jobs for all the boys. After examining the youth situation in early 1961, Bourguiba exclaimed: "What I have discovered is awful."[8] It was revealed that no more than 100,000 out of 2 million Tunisians under the age of twenty are now affiliated with any of the organizations;* in 1959 only 2,383 were involved in specific programs of the Neo-Destour Youth, although tens of thousands more had some contact with the party branches. After Bour-

* Few students are now active in their union, UGET, perhaps because it is so closely linked with the party. (In the annual elections of the Paris section, in May, 1963 a majority turned up to outvote the party candidates, but the elections were then nullified.) UTIC in 1960 was down to 20,000 members, half of its 1948 membership. The UGTT, which had claimed

guiba's speech, efforts were made to form a well-trained elite consisting of ten youths to a branch. It was hoped that these 10,000 young people would constitute an active, dedicated minority to set the example for the rest of Tunisia and provide future organizing cadres. Experiments, too, were started to train selected youths in agricultural cooperatives, which they would later own. If the experiments should succeed, they may provide one answer for staffing the cooperatives projected in Tunisia's Plan.

It seems virtually impossible to evaluate the impact made on the masses by Neo-Destour activity, but the party obviously facilitates the execution of specific government projects by explaining their purpose to the local population. The farmer on a mountain slope is made to understand why the government must plant trees on his property, and the cart driver can be made to see why he must replace metal with rubber wheels. Although party exhortations may have made the farmer more willing to listen to the advice of the agricultural expert, it remains that progress is slow without the experts. After decades of exposure to nationalist opposition politics, the city dweller and the Sahel peasant are not blindly obedient to government policies; they require the political explanations that the Neo-Destour is able to give. The party's educational efforts are aided by a genuine social consensus on the value of education. This greatly facilitates the other role of the party—helping to create responsible citizens—a role that complements its function in mobilizing the masses behind the programs of the government.

182,000 members in 1956, probably did not have more than 65,000 dues-paying members in 1960.

The party has also suffered a loss in membership, perhaps because of its very success. Membership has dwindled to half what it was in 1955 in some of its traditional strongholds, and probably amounts now to no more than 250,000—still roughly one-quarter of the adult male population.

4. How Much Democracy?

An articulate Neo-Destour militant, no matter how modest his schooling, almost invariably punctuates his remarks, whether about economic development or the prospects of democracy in Tunisia, with the comment: "You know, we are living in a period of transition." The educated party member usually adds, when asked about the Neo-Destour's monopoly of power, that he hopes competitive parties will emerge eventually, but that national unity is needed at present to confront Tunisia's gigantic problems of development.

The single-party system is clearly not democratic. There is no effective opposition party to check the people in power. Within the party, there is no democratic process in the sense that two or more groups compete at all levels under accepted ground rules. Even factions remain highly fluid as individuals compete for Bourguiba's favor.

The Tunisian regime, however, is not antidemocratic or totalitarian. The Neo-Destour and its national organizations are fairly representative of the nation. If the people are not as enthusiastic about the regime now as during the honeymoon after independence, they still give their tacit consent. The Neo-Destour does not use repression or foster a climate of mutual suspicion in order to maintain itself in power. It does not have a rigid ideology which it must force people to believe, and it does not invade the privacy of the home. The Neo-Destour is sufficiently secure not to require totalitarian methods to keep itself in power.

If an authoritarian regime is to be a tutelary democracy, it must, while bringing about the social and economic conditions requisite for democracy, fulfill a number of political conditions. Negatively, it must avoid repressive methods so far as possible. In a more positive sense, it should respect democratic forms.

If democratic traditions are to take root, authority must be open to constructive criticism. This can only be accomplished through the rational discussion, undistorted by demagogy or messianic ideology, of both national and local problems. In order to impart to the whole society the democratic aspirations and values of the elite, a multitude of well-informed citizens must be educated. Above all, widespread participation in local political affairs— together with a developing interrelationship between local and national politics—seems to be the basic precondition for democratic growth. Perhaps little more should be asked of a regime whose main task is to ensure the cohesion of the nation in a period of difficult social and economic adjustment. In fact, the Tunisian record in local political life is much more promising of healthy democratic growth than the picture presented by political practices at the national level.

National Politics

Bourguiba constantly stresses that he is a democrat who believes in the dignity of the individual. But however enlightened, he rules like a monarch and appeals directly to the people, rather than to institutions, for support. Although he needs an organization like the Neo-Destour to sustain his mass appeal, he seems to have wanted to limit its real influence in the affairs of state. In national politics there was until 1963 little criticism of authority, a minimum of public discussion except on technical matters, and an evident devaluation of potentially democratic structures.

Bourguiba stands above all criticism, for to criticize him is tantamount to criticizing the state he personifies. If the Neo-Destour had set up a constitutional monarchy instead of deposing the bey, Bourguiba would have been more exposed to criticism inside the party or within the party-controlled National Assembly. As it is, these forums only rarely challenge in public the work even of the subordinates in Bourguiba's Cabinet. Although there is no press censorship, the daily newspapers and the radio must obey the instructions of the Ministry of Information or face suspension. The only public criticism of authority in the early 1960's came from the monthly Communist-inspired paper *Tribune du Progrès,* which interested only a small circle of intellectuals and was eventually banned.

The history of *L'Action* and its successors illustrates the amount of even constructive criticism permitted by the regime. *L'Action* was a weekly newspaper in the French language started in 1955 by a team of young journalists under the patronage of Mohamed Masmoudi. Although not an official organ of the Neo-Destour, its ties with the party were close. Masmoudi was a favorite of Bourguiba and a member of the Political Bureau; the editor, Bechir Ben Yahmed, was in charge of the Ministry of Information in 1956.

In early 1957, the loyal weekly incurred Bourguiba's wrath by contrasting his government's achievements with its promises of early municipal elections and rigorous recruitment by merit in the administration—"All this is important to the extent that it is the little nothings which spoil great things"[1]—and by broaching the subject of Cabinet shuffles. Bourguiba made a speech criticizing "storytellers harbored by friendly papers" who "sow trouble in people's minds" by talk of Cabinet changes,[2] and *L'Action* ceased publication for a week. The paper praised the President the following week, but complained of being "up against the hostility and intolerance of all those—numerous and powerful—who conceive of liberty only as a one-way street."[3]

L'Action lambasted the Constituent Assembly—which was to stall three years before drafting a constitution—for its "interminable monologues that are called debates."[4] The paper then carried out a poll on popular attitudes toward the government from which they learned that 44 per cent believed the government had made mistakes.[5] Two weeks later it described the activities of the Neo-Destour Youth as "a pretty clumsy parody of Scouting," whose monthly publication was designed less for Tunisian youth than as propaganda for Middle Eastern countries.

In the summer of 1958, *L'Action* criticized the regime's show trials of the collaborationist elite: "This measure of public house-cleaning was necessary . . . [but] would have gained by being started earlier and now should be ended rapidly and clearly, according to the rules."[6] As the trials dragged on—they were to last until February, 1959, and convict scores of people—*L'Action's* tone became more vehement. When Tahar Ben Ammar, the Prime Minister of Tunisia's transitional government just before independence, was brought to trial for "plotting" with the bey, *L'Action* exploded: "Nasty little quarrels, pettiness on all sides, an absence of principles or perspective, have been spread in the pages of our newspapers and on our radio waves, creating a general feeling of uneasiness and equivocation."[7]

On the same day, the Political Bureau withdrew its support of the paper and accused it of "confusing the public by systematically denigrating the policy of President Bourguiba's Government and attacking the fundamental institutions of the republican regime."[8] Masmoudi was removed five days later from the party's Political Bureau, after his only defender, Mongi Slim, had departed for his United Nations post. The episode marked the end for several years of non-Communist criticism of Tunisia's internal affairs.

Ben Yahmed's paper was resurrected under the name of *Afrique-Action* in October, 1960, but was designed to discuss African rather than internal Tunisian affairs. When, after a year, it started indirectly to criticize Bourguiba, the paper was humbled under interesting circumstances.

Bourguiba's gamble at Bizerte had painfully backfired. The pressure of public opinion, as shown by mass demonstrations and blockades of the bases, and even the moral pressure of a United Nations resolution, had failed to budge France from Bizerte. Bourguiba's friends in the West, taken by surprise, gave Tunisia no apparent support. Led in the days following the fighting to seek the support of the Afro-Asian bloc, Bourguiba's actions seemed to justify the pan-Arab slogans once used by Ben Youssef, who was assassinated in August. When, in September, Bourguiba blatantly misconstrued a speech of De Gaulle's in order to hand the General an olive branch, Tunisians who had been aroused by the spirit of national sacrifice, the rapprochement with Egypt, and Belgrade neutralism questioned Bourguiba's judgment. In this general context of Bourguiba's slipping prestige, *Afrique-Action* wrote its barbed editorial about *"pouvoir personnel."*

Accompanied by a picture of King Farouk (Masmoudi had just returned from Egypt, where he praised Nasser for continuing to live in his modest army officer's house), the editorial seemed less a general description of personal regimes in Africa than an accurate dig at Bourguiba's republic:

> In the twentieth century one witnesses, rather than the abolition of monarchy, its transformation into a power that differs from it only in two ways: it is not given by birth, it is taken (and therefore must be kept); it is not handed down and therefore raises permanently the problem of succession. It is the *pouvoir personnel.*
>
> . . . .
>
> Today Bourguiba holds more power, legally and actually, than did the Bey and Resident General together. . . . All rival forces are . . . dislocated, subjugated, or eliminated: the judiciary, a deliberative assembly, trade unions or political parties, and the press continue to exist, but their liberty of action no longer exists. . . . They constitute nothing more than supporting instruments of the Power, which addresses itself without an intermediary to the people. Everything converges toward the holder of power who alone exists, decides, and in expressing himself expresses the country and incarnates it.
>
> In the orbit of the Power others can benefit from a certain consideration or play a role. Outside there is no possibility.
>
> The police is not all-powerful, but it is omnipresent. Imprisonment without trial exists but is used more as a means of intimidation. Anyone can be arrested, but the prisons are not full. That is to say, *pouvoir personnel* is not dictatorship. . . . It is a permanent compromise between democracy, difficult and unrealizable in some situations, and dictatorship.
>
> . . . .
>
> Because it develops arrogance and contempt on the part of the leader, docility and servility on the part of the led, it is in itself a threat to the moral health of a people.[9]

Bourguiba's response was cleverly delayed and devastating. He went ahead with a contemplated Cabinet shift, and Masmoudi declined the humiliating offer to become ambassador to a minor African country. The Neo-Destour organ, *El Amal,* printed a series of editorials admitting that the regime had not yet solved the Bizerte crisis, or persuaded everyone to back the Plan, or rectified abuses by the police.[10] But the editorials vigorously defended Bourguiba and the Neo-Destour militants. A polemic ensued between *Afrique-Action* and *El Amal,* while some militants at party cadres' conferences questioned the "aggressive attitude of *Afrique-Action.*"[11] With the ground well prepared, the Political Bureau again banished Masmoudi but allowed the paper to continue to appear under a different name, *Jeune-Afrique,* limiting it to an exclusively African role. Masmoudi, publicly tongue-lashed by Bourguiba, was relegated to the political wilderness; in the municipal elections of 1963, he was not even permitted to run for re-election as mayor of Mahdia.

Five weeks after the famous editorial, Ben Yahmed was refining his analysis of *pouvoir personnel:*

> There are different types of *pouvoir personnel.* That which Bourguiba holds in Tunisia has been produced by History. It imposed itself naturally. Tunisians have welcomed it and—as we have—supported it.
> Today we believe that Bourguiba's style of *pouvoir personnel* is one of the best, that it is adapted to the present situation in Tunisia, but that it must evolve. It is our duty as conscientious Tunisians to suggest to our countrymen the direction which this evolution should take.

Pouvoir personnel, Ben Yahmed went on to say, can save the country if it avoids becoming a totalitarian dictatorship and if, at the same time, it prepares for succession by "leading the country by stages toward a structured democracy, that is to say by establishing republican institutions."[12] In March, 1963, after seven years of independence and national consolidation, Bourguiba was to respond to Ben Yahmed's challenge.

Bourguiba's forceful rule had reduced the importance not only of the National Assembly but of the party itself. To subordinate the party to the state was probably not in itself harmful to democracy, for this ensured that educated "technicians" in the administration—and therefore citizens at large—would be somewhat protected from the jealousy and exactions of veteran militants unfit for power. But the reorganization of the party structures in 1958 also paralyzed its deliberative organs. The National Congress was not convened in late 1957 because the leaders were contemplating its reorganization. In 1959, it met to ratify the structural changes, among them the provision that the Congress meet every three years. In 1962, however, the leaders delayed convening the Congress in order to avoid any embarrassing discussions about Bizerte. Instead, they called a meeting of the National Council to discuss only the Plan. The National Council, in theory to meet every three months, was called on schedule only in January and June of 1956. It met again in April, 1957, and then was discontinued until 1962.*

The fifteen members of the Political Bureau—theoretically elected by the National Congress, but sometimes coopted—supposedly met informally once a week over Bourguiba's dinner table. They seemed, however, to have all but lost their role as policy-makers. Almost half of them were either figureheads or absent from the country too regularly to keep in close contact. Day-to-day decisions about both party and government affairs were in the hands of three or four men. It was only in times of crisis or when a very important decision was taken that the Political Bureau held a formal meeting with most of its members present. In theory, the Bureau was to decide upon important lines of policy, which the "technicians" of Bourguiba's Cabinet would then execute; in practice, the Bureau became little more than one of Bourguiba's innumerable vehicles of consultation. He used it as circumstances dictated, since its support provided politically useful protection.

To be sure, the sporadic discussion and debates of Congresses and National Councils injected a democratic atmosphere into

* It was claimed that a more democratically elected National Council would compensate for the suppression of the federation and their annual congresses. (See *Petit Matin*, March 5, 1959.) While the old National Council had consisted of the members of the Political Bureau, the heads of the federations, and an equal number of militants elected by the National Congress, the new Council was to consist mostly of delegates elected directly by the branches.

the party's otherwise bureaucratized structure. The unanimous agreements and applause gave evidence of national solidarity. That Bourguiba and his lieutenants took the need for the delegates' approval seriously was illustrated by their very caution in convening the assemblies. Discussion was free. Family bickering—harassing a Cabinet member for hours with penetrating questions—was permitted in these reunions, so long as the prestige of the father figure was not questioned. Surprises occurred, as when the delegates to the 1959 Congress demonstrated their distaste for Bourguiba's personal entourage by refusing to re-elect one of its key members to the Political Bureau.

It was clear to most party militants, however, that the deliberative organs of the party led a marginal existence. There seemed to be little or no relation between the discussion of the rank and file in regional and local assemblies and the national process. The desire of the militants to have a more effective dialogue with the hierarchy was increased as a result of the abortive plot on Bourguiba's life in December, 1962,* and the increasingly authoritarian political atmosphere prevailing in early 1963.

With the sense of timing for which he is famous, Bourguiba, on March 2, abruptly bridged the widening gulf between the militants and his government. At a meeting of the National Council—the second one within a year—he called upon the party to overhaul its structures so as to give the militants a greater voice in national affairs. After three days of discussion, the National Council proposed the following changes: (1) active membership in the party would be restricted to those who had proved their competence and loyalty, although the party would remain open to all Tunisians; (2) the Commissioner would be

* The group that planned the assassination seemed to be an assortment of Youssefists (wishing to avenge the assassination of their leader), a few army officers, and former *fellagha* leaders whose transport licenses and other patronage spoils were being taken away by a government intent on rational economic planning. On January 18, 1963, Tunisia broke off diplomatic relations with Algeria, which was harboring some of the plotters. There seems no reason to suppose however, either that the Ben Bella Government was encouraging a change of regime in Tunisia, or that the plotters were an organized political group with a program that could gain domestic support. By March, relations between Tunisia and Algeria had begun to improve.

replaced by a Regional Coordinating Committee elected by the branches and headed by an elected General Secretary; (3) the Political Bureau would be enlarged into a forty- or fifty-man elected Central Committee; (4) Bourguiba would appoint a five- or six-man Party Executive. The Political Bureau was mandated to institute these sweeping changes, which the National Congress of 1964 would then ratify.

In a sense, the party was to become even less democratic at the top, since an appointed Executive would replace the Political Bureau; but the change only formalized long-standing practice. Potentially of much greater significance was the fact that the party now had three deliberative organs—the Congress, the National Council, and the Central Committee—at the national level, and democratically elected organs at the regional as well as local levels. If the reforms are effectively carried out, the party will have every prospect of developing an institutionalized democratic process under Bourguiba's tutelage. Possibly a mechanism may develop not only for discussing national policy but also for providing an acceptable successor when Bourguiba eventually retires.

The other structure with a democratic potential is the National Assembly. Tunisia's top leaders are in this ninety-man body. Forty-one of them have, at one time or another since independence, held important political positions.* In addition, some of the national and regional leaders of the national organizations are also deputies, so that more than half can be considered professional politicians. The only group comparable in political experience was the Neo-Destour's National Council of 1955–57. The deputies' educational background is also impressive. Thirty-one had completed their studies at French universities, while an additional twenty-five had received at least a modern secondary-school education. Their geographic origins reflect the political dominance of Tunis and the Sahel.

* Twelve have been members of the Political Bureau; seventeen are or have been Cabinet members; seven are currently or have been party commissioners; four are former governors, and one is Director of Bourguiba's private Cabinet.

Although the National Assembly gathers together the core of Tunisia's political elite, its powers are severely limited. During the six months each year that it is convened, it meets in fact only about fifteen times in plenary session. Legislation is discussed mostly in the secrecy of the Assembly's standing commissions. Deputies may propose legislation, but thus far the Assembly has discussed only Presidential proposals. As often as not, laws have been made by Presidential decree when the Assembly is not in session, and have been subsequently ratified. The Assembly may overrule a Presidential veto by two-thirds majority, but such a situation seems politically inconceivable. Its internal organization helps to assure discipline and subservience to the government.*

Discussion in plenary is almost nonexistent. The chairman of the relevant standing commission reads his report, and after brief comments the legislation is usually passed unanimously. Cabinet members may attend the plenary, but debate, if any, is focused on the specific piece of legislation rather than on general policy. Usually full discussion with Cabinet members in the privacy of the standing commissions will have already produced agreement in favor of the legislation. Only during the three or four days a year when the budget is discussed do deputies have the opportunity publicly to question and criticize the government's programs—which does not prevent the budget from being passed without amendments.

In 1961, even before the issues of Bizerte and *pouvoir personnel* enlivened the political scene, the deputies were beginning to show modest signs of being more than Bourguiba's rubber stamp. On a close vote they decided to return to commission a decree law, actively defended in plenary by Bourguiba's spokesman, Bahi Ladgham, and the Minister of Agriculture. Three weeks later, on a significant point of procedure, the deputies successfully rebelled against the President of the Assembly.

* A nine-man Assembly Bureau, headed by a member of the Political Bureau, is elected annually, but the party decides who is to be elected. The Bureau controls the Assembly's agenda and coordinates the work of the standing commissions; its president, like a schoolteacher in class, opens and closes debate as he pleases.

They rejected his package proposal to ratify ten decree laws and insisted instead upon a separate law for each decree. The President accepted this five days later, after he had closed the short and stormy debate to have time "to think over the suggested proposal."

Despite the slight increase of parliamentary activity, the National Assembly remains politically subordinate to Bourguiba, and serves only as a consultative mechanism and as a distinguished audience to applaud the President's occasional addresses. Like the party's deliberative organs which have fallen into disuse, the Assembly is important only for its potential as a democratic institution.

Local Politics

In contrast to the national scene, a healthy democratic political process flourishes at the local level, especially in Tunis and the Sahel. Through its decades of experience, the party has developed a network of branches that transcend traditional local rivalries while providing democratic structures. Local democracy, of course, has its limits; Tunisians do not yet have the political maturity of the colonial New Englander. But the branches do more than mobilize the people in support of government projects; they represent the people and give them the opportunity to manage many of their local affairs. They also train citizens to participate constructively in national affairs.

One of the party's greatest achievements has been to organize its 1,000 branches along rational geographic lines. Each branch represents a population that may be divided by traditional tribal, village, or extended family rivalries, and thus helps to diminish ancient antipathies. But such enmities are still very much a part of Tunisia's political landscape. Even in the politically sophisticated Sahel, a long-standing rivalry between two villages less than a mile apart once forced the Neo-Destour to set up two organizations, and in some of the larger villages, separate branches were established to satisfy antipathetic family groups settled in different parts of the same town. In southern mining towns, the party could group together workers from diverse tribes only with the help of the UGTT. Today's rationalized local structure holds rival factions together, but strong central supervision is often needed to keep the branches from splitting apart under the strain.

The local branches operate like modern voluntary associations. Membership is open to all Tunisians living in the branch's area, although the Executive Committee may turn down a prospective member. Membership is rarely a demanding activity. Apart from attending the annual assembly and information meetings every three months, the member is committed only to respecting the principles of the party, executing its decisions, and paying his dues—at least in part. Active participation in branch activities is limited to the eight to twelve members of the Executive Committee, who meet at least once every two weeks. Members of the Executive Committee may also choose promising militants to act on various committees unofficially set up to assist the busy officers. Some of the more active branches in Tunis claim up to fifty hard-working activists, including propagandists in all the local cafés.

The local branches are under the tutelage of the Political Commissioner in each governorate, a supervisor equipped with many powers that his elected successor, the General Secretary of the Regional Coordinating Committee, will most likely inherit. He transmits orders and programs to the branches from the Political Bureau's propaganda, youth, financial, and social-development services. With access to police reports and confidential party sources, he screens candidates for the elections to the branch Executive Committee. With the assent of the Political Bureau, he may discipline any branch officer or member, or dissolve the entire Executive Committee, replace it by appointed officers, and arrange new elections within six months. He may also divide or regroup existing branches.

The branch's Executive Committee is freely elected each year. The Commissioner rarely turns down a prospective candidate, though when he does, the candidate usually hesitates to exercise his right to challenge the judgment of the Commissioner. There are almost invariably more candidates than positions to fill, but the same officers usually are re-elected. There seems to be no systematic effort, even on the part of members close to the Commissioner, to elect a fixed slate. Voting patterns are usually irregular, although fifty women members of a branch in Sousse once voted as a bloc and swung the balance to the incumbents.* (In urban branches, where the large majority is literate, voting is by secret ballot on a single list, and secrecy is maintained even in the rural assemblies of illiterate voters.) The elected committee then allots the various offices to its members, usually in consultation with the Commissioner or his representative.

The democratically elected Executive Committee usually functions adequately, unless it is paralyzed by rival factions, which generally stem from competing families in the community. The Commissioner rarely exercises his disciplinary powers: In 1960, only 6 out of the 120 branches in the Sousse area presented problems serious enough to give the Commissioner cause to suspend their executive committees. In the party as a whole there are seldom more than a dozen cases a year of disciplinary measures applied to individuals. In fact, well-functioning branches have more autonomy than the hierarchical structure of the party might suggest. Especially in the Sahel, where branch leaders often have connections with leading national figures, the Commissioner must exercise diplomacy and restraint. In some villages, figures on the national level exercise active leadership. Even a Cabinet member as busy as Ben Salah usually spends one Sunday every month in his home town, where he is the mayor and president of the branch, and Bourguiba has a passionate interest in everything concerning Monastir, although he passed on the mayorship to his son in 1963.

One of the branch's primary roles is to represent local aspirations and grievances to the higher authorities. The branch officer in charge of "social development" is, among other things, responsible for discovering and expressing the specific needs of the

* Outside the main cities, few women belong to the party. But in 1960, the Union Nationale des Femmes Tunisiennes (UNFT) claimed 40,000 adult members and 5,000 girls associated with the Neo-Destour Youth.

population to the Commissioner. Roughly once a year, the Commissioner arranges meetings with the Governor, his technicians from the various administrations, and the branch officers. Technical priorities are explained to the branches, but government action is sometimes also modified in light of branch needs.

In rural areas the branch may have access to the government through the local sheik, an appointed administrative official, who will often have been the former president of the branch. The Governor's Delegate to the government (the sheik's administrative superior) also keeps in constant touch with the branch leaders, though in theory the administrations of party and government meet only at the level of Commissioner and Governor. The Governor's Delegate, though possibly a stranger to the region, is almost invariably a veteran party militant. He may need the good will of the branch officers in order to carry out his government projects more effectively, and the officers may find it useful to make suggestions to the Delegate as well as to the Commissioner. The latter exercises a balancing influence on conflicting claims and may ease tensions that arise between the citizens and the administration; his power to satisfy particular demands is an important lever for obtaining efficiency and harmony in the localities.*

The branch is usually the center of local government in rural areas, where it overshadows the sheik. In most villages and towns of more than a few thousand inhabitants, the town councils, instituted in 1957, have significantly extended the responsibilities of many branch leaders, who have almost invariably been elected

---

* The branches used to serve as local employment bureaus. Immediately after independence, anyone who wanted a job, either as a street cleaner or as director of a lucrative transportation company, had to be a Neo-Destourian. The local branch was usually the definitive judge of the applicant's political past, and the prime function of the federation was to find jobs for deserving militants. Though in general no longer permitted to discriminate against nonparty elements in the population, the branch continues to have some patronage. For instance, it hands out cards to the needy to qualify them for certain public benefits. Much to the embarrassment of the Ministry of Education, it may even keep nonparty children out of the school canteens or out of the few primary schools built exclusively by its labor and fund-raising activities.

to the town council. In small villages, the town council and branch may be virtually identical in composition. Where they are distinct, it is the branch's task to articulate criticism and to mobilize popular support for the projects of the council.

Whereas the town councils have limited authority and inadequate financial resources, the party's branch officers and militants are in a position to acquire the arts of leadership and assimilate a generally democratic political style. They inform the branch membership of all aspects of town planning and organize mass meetings. Confronted with various local situations, they are constantly faced with practical problems and with learning new skills: A young branch president in Tunis, with little formal schooling beyond primary school, suddenly found himself in charge of a glass factory, his branch's special project in the battle against underdevelopment, and had to learn his economics as he had once learned politics, by practical experience. The local cadres constitute an elite being trained by the party for local, regional, and even national responsibilities. The man in charge of the glass factory, for instance, has become the Tunis Commissioner's right-hand man.

In occupational background, the cadres, or branch officers, are a very mixed group, reflecting the population at large. There are roughly 10,000 of them; however, if one includes all the more active branch members, local political activities provide roughly 50,000 Tunisians with some tangible role in managing their own public affairs. Due largely to social environment and recent political history, the quality of the cadres is best in the cities and in the Sahel.

It is significant, however, that an inquiry made by this writer in 1960 in the Sahel reveals a large proportion of illiterate people among the party cadres; only 1 per cent had a modern university degree, only one-fifth claimed any sort of secondary education, and one-sixth any primary-school education. (However, 29 per cent claimed the ability to read and write, despite the lack of formal schooling.) The proportion of uneducated people is probably still higher in other provinces. But lack of formal education is somewhat offset by years of experience within the party: The records indicated that more than one-third of the cadres joined before 1942. Their occupational backgrounds clearly indicate the representative character of the party leadership at the local level: If one-twelfth were schoolteachers and less than 2 per cent high-school professors, doctors, or upper-echelon officials, more than one quarter were townspeople following various occupations—from clockmaker to café waiter—while another 7 per cent worked at low-level administrative posts. More than half were simply farmers, for the most part of very modest means.

Seasoned cadres, while maintaining their local sources of authority, have often been attuned to modern ideas and social change. For instance, Zitouna-trained schoolmasters have sometimes been heard to advocate birth control as a partial answer to the Sahel's economic problems. Their word undoubtedly has more weight than that of a university-trained outsider.

Entree to the ranks of the party elite is theoretically open to anyone who can get himself elected to a branch committee. But in ancient villages and in the old quarters of the cities, "outsiders" usually cannot be elected, even if they have worked in the area for years. Except in recently created communities, the imported village schoolteacher is considered a foreigner, although he may come from a neighboring town. With the diplomatic support of the Commissioner, however, he may achieve local standing and get elected to the branch committee.

The party cadres have had regular opportunities to participate in national politics, although not through the party's formal organization. Besides calling meetings of branch officers to help decide upon the party's various regional programs, the Commissioners developed, from 1960 to 1963, the informal practice of calling cadres' conferences three or four times a year to discuss national policies.

The cadres' conferences did not quite take the place of the old annual federation congresses, nor did they fill the vacuum left by the devaluation of the party's top deliberative organs; there was no structured debate followed by voting of resolutions that might commit the party's leadership to particular courses of action. But the conferences ensured that the cadres have some feeling of participation and even a measure of influence in national policy-making. After a member of the Political Bureau, who often presided over the conference, delivered his opening speech, the floor was open to questions. The commissioner encouraged the cadres to be critical. Questions and comments revealed the problems that are of the greatest concern to the rank and file and showed the leaders at least where to concentrate party propaganda. Often, too, a Political Bureau member like Ben Salah might use comments made by the cadres as arguments to other leaders in support of his controversial ideas. The cadres' conferences, in short, were the regime's one major forum where the rank and file might confront the leaders on matters of national substance. In this respect, the party not only served as a training ground for local leadership but also broadened its participation in national affairs.

Obviously, democratic institutions—and even the democratic idea—are young in Tunisia. Ultimately, representative democracy demands accepted procedures for deciding upon alternative policies and leaders. Tunisia has not yet reached this stage, and indeed is in many respects more nearly a monarchy than a democracy. The regime seems, however, to be playing an interesting role as a tutelary democracy. Political participation has been meaningfully extended to the masses, and democratic forms are generally respected on the local level. Active citizens are being trained in the branches, where rational discussion and constructive criticism are encouraged. Moreover, the Neo-Destour has extended political participation in national politics, first through the cadres' conferences and now through more effective use of regional and national deliberative organs elected by the mass membership. Although Bourguiba had no preconceived plan for democratic development, the reforms of 1963 follow a certain logic: The single-party regime, which first fostered local democracy, is now attempting to extend the new styles into a more broadly based national political process.

The regime, of course, is transitional and still depends upon

Bourguiba's presence. He could perhaps do more to activate national institutions such as the National Assembly. *Pouvoir personnel* at times seems to undermine the party's democratic ethos. On the other hand, the national cohesion needed to launch a new country is probably always incompatible in the short run with the development of democratic institutions as they developed in the West. In the long run, this very cohesion, by providing a framework for economic and social progress by persuasion rather than coercion, may produce a society where representative democracy is practicable. Meanwhile, political institutions are developing that may someday be able to function independently of their creator.

The single-party system in Tunisia, and perhaps in other new countries, can be most usefully understood as a compromise that reflects the predicament of the transitional society. Many of the elements of the society are unprepared to take part fully in the political process. If the party is sufficiently open and its elite sufficiently homogeneous, however, most of those who can take part are given the opportunity. At the same time, the more backward masses are gradually brought into politics through the local party, where they are encouraged to discuss the problems with which they are most familiar. The single-party system in Tunisia can thus be called a tutelary democracy. The activities of the Neo-Destour at the local and regional levels suggest that Bourguiba's vision of a modern democratic society is being partially reconciled with the realities of the single party's monopoly of political power.

A new style of national politics, possibly more dependent upon institutions, will begin after Bourguiba retires, but his presence seems needed as the regime begins its experiment in planning. The history of Bourguibism suggests that a controlled social and economic revolution may be accomplished without precluding individual freedom.

III. Social and Economic Change

CHARLES A. MICAUD

1. A Strategy of Modernization?

If successful modernization means a more rational use of economic resources, the introduction of modern tools and methods, and priority given to the most productive types of investment, then the Tunisian experiment can hardly be considered a success. The economy remained stagnant five years after independence. Few new industries were started. Public and private investments were lower than in the preindependence days. Little was done to improve production and productivity. In 1959, less than one-seventh of Tunisia's imports consisted of capital goods; more private cars and luxury items were imported than trucks and machinery. The few innovations, as those in the field of credit, for example, do not fit a careful blueprint but appear to be *ad hoc* improvisations. An empirical and conservative approach to economic problems has been the rule. While encouraging private initiative, the government, until 1961, avoided systematic coordination of efforts.

By contrast, a massive effort has been made to transform attitudes and values and to reduce psychological and social obstacles to progress. Investment in human resources has outstripped investment in capital goods. New schools, not factories, have multiplied. A true social and psychological revolution has taken place, marked by such radical reforms as the liberation of women from the autocratic rule of father and husband, the redistribution of land through the elimination of the religious *habous,* and the thorough reform of the educational system at a cost that seems disproportionately high in view of the existing resources. One may add to the list the alleviation of unemployment through the institution of work camps, which are more a social than an economically sound investment.

Several explanations have been offered to account for the imbalance between social change and economic development. The first explanation is that the imbalance is due to the existence of a class struggle between the bourgeoisie and the urban proletariat. The position of the proletariat was presented by Ahmed Ben Salah, Secretary of the General Union of Tunisian Workers, in his report to the union in 1956. "Neither the individual or the citizen, nor the collectivity or the people, can be reformed except in the framework of a profound revolution of economic structures, for it is on these structures in the last analysis that society rests."[1] This revolutionary approach was rejected by the government, which resulted in Ben Salah's prompt removal from his leadership of the UGTT. Is this incident to be interpreted as a significant victory for the bourgeoisie, which dominated the political scene in Tunisia until 1961? This is what as cautious a scholar as Moncef Guen seems to imply when he states that "despite the dominant climate of social peace and a formula of class collaboration adopted by all groups, it is nevertheless true that the bourgeoisie was the victor in the test of strength from 1954 to 1957, for it had two main assets: money and, especially, education."[2] Guen makes two reservations, however; he points out that the Tunisian bourgeoisie is not reactionary, and that great social mobility permits access to important positions in the administration by qualified people, whatever their social origin.

It is difficult, in fact, to apply Marxist categories to the Tunisian situation and to find in class struggle an explanation for the lack of systematic economic reforms. The Tunisian bourgeoisie hardly fits into the Marxist concept of capitalism, for only 10 per cent of private industry is owned and operated by Tunisians. Native investors continue to show great reluctance to accept risks, and prefer the safer outlets of land ownership and commerce. But this commercial and landowning bourgeoisie is small and of much less consequence than the new intellectual elite, which stems from the bourgeoisie as well as from the lower middle class of peasant proprietors, artisans, and shopkeepers. Some elements of this elite, perhaps a majority, may have conservative attitudes, but the group itself has no vested interest in the economic *status quo*. Nor can the workers in mines and industry be considered disposed toward class struggle, despite their organization in trade unions and the aggressiveness of some of their leaders. The real proletariat has been mainly rural. Particularly numerous in the Center and the South of the country, it is unorganized and helpless.

Nor was the political situation in 1956 conducive to class war. The party and administration offered enough outlets to talent to rob dissatisfied social groups of leadership. The party itself had a monopoly of power and acted as an efficient arbiter of conflicting group interests. Obviously, the need for consolidating the framework of the new independent state precluded social warfare. As Guen points out, the government needed, above all, to keep the cohesion of the social forces: "President Bourguiba had already estimated that Tunisia could not afford the luxury of domestic struggle, which appeared to him not only fratricidal but certain to lead the country away from the fight against the vestiges of colonialism."[3] In 1956, Guen states, "Grave political problems faced the country: the concretization of a purely nominal independence, the evacuation of French bases, frontier incidents, and the need to establish and consolidate the new institutional framework."[4]

Gabriel Ardant, a French observer of Tunisia's modernization efforts, offers a variation on the theme of bourgeois dominance. Writing in 1961, he pointed out that the concerns of the Tunisian dominant class have been essentially those of the European bourgeoisie of the eighteenth and nineteenth centuries: Faith in progress, reason, and science have been translated into efforts to liberate the mind from the shackles of the past and to eliminate obstacles to the self-realization and happiness of the individual. In Ardant's opinion, the emancipation of women and the granting of property rights on *habous* lands correspond to the reforms accomplished by the French Revolution, and the growth of modern secular education to the interests of the nineteenth-century champions of reason and progress. Will this bourgeoisie, he asked, be ready now to face the realities of the twentieth century and accept the need for maximum technological development and for a rational organization of the economy, involving decisions concerning priorities, and hence national planning?

Will the Tunisian bourgeoisie be able to transcend its own class interests, accept the necessary sacrifices, and help build a new society?[5]

This analysis in terms of class interests and class conflict is typical of the approach of some intellectuals who, quite naturally, apply to newly independent countries the categories with which they are familiar and often have to stretch the reality to fit the categories. Given the fact that the terms "bourgeoisie" and "proletariat" have little meaning in the Tunisian situation, class consciousness could have been aroused only by the persistent and effective propaganda of an active Communist Party. This was not the case. The workers had, long before independence, given their allegiance to the nationalist UGTT, itself closely tied to the Neo-Destour Party. When independence came, the ties were maintained and the unions were committed to continued cooperation with the party, even at the sacrifice of earlier expectations. The leitmotiv was the cooperation of all groups for the construction of the new nation-state, and not class struggle —the Ben Salah episode notwithstanding.

Other explanations must be sought to account for the postponing of economic development and the emphasis put on social reform. There are several possible explanations, perhaps complementary. The first, and most obvious, is the wisdom of concentrating on social reforms, including education, before embarking upon a policy of systematic economic reforms. Under the strategy of change adopted by the government, priority had to be given to the elimination of social and psychological obstacles to progress and to the creation of an adequately skilled labor force. A systematic mobilization of resources demanded time to gather statistical data, to draw up careful estimates of needed priorities, to recruit and train administrative and managerial talent, and to gain the support of popular opinion. Such a vast effort could not be embarked upon lightly. The first steps were undertaken as early as 1957 and led to the ten-year programs of development in education and agriculture, as well as to the creation of a National Planning Council in 1959.

Moreover, the achievement of political independence had not freed the country of its economic ties with France; total economic independence had to come in stages if serious disturbances were to be avoided. As Tunisian leaders openly proclaimed, the first duty of the government was to consolidate the finances of the new state, the prerequisite for effective independence.

In the climate created by the Algerian War, a cautious wait-and-see approach to economic problems was all the more necessary. Concentration on social problems offered several advantages: It paved the way for future economic growth, did not depend for its success on foreign economic aid, and avoided the dangerous issue of the foreign ownership of land and factories. It was necessary not to antagonize France, and equally necessary to reassure foreign and domestic investors. The government offered credit and tax advantages to would-be investors and the President urged potential entrepreneurs to accept some risks. The government even attempted to play the role of the *entrepreneur-pilote*, launching new enterprises in order to encourage timid investors. But it soon became obvious that foreign capital would not move into Tunisia and that Tunisians would persist in their traditional ways of acquiring and accumulating wealth. Finally, the profit-making motive had to give way to the concept of national planning; in the absence of individual initiative, savings had to be channeled into investments whose priority was established by the planners.

In the years following independence it was essential to strengthen social and political cohesion by avoiding issues—such as economic planning—that would be likely to create serious opposition. The foremost objective was the consolidation of the new state. By concentrating on the goal of modernization, and avoiding the ticklish problem of the methods of achieving it, one could create a nearly unanimous feeling that progress was desirable. Progress could be used as a unifying symbol, as well as the battering ram against the strongholds of traditionalism that had to be toppled to make way for the modern nation-state.

Progress also involved the conflict of two desirable goals whose clash is perhaps inherent in the process of decolonization—the conflict between the goal of total and immediate independence on the one hand and the goal of rapid modernization on the other. There seems to be little doubt that in the mind of Bourguiba the latter was not to be sacrificed to the former. When internal autonomy was promised in 1954, he apparently told Mendès-France that total independence could wait ten years. Successful modernization demanded continued close ties with France, ensuring a constant influx of capital and technological and managerial know-how. Economic development would come not from the total mobilization of meager national resources but from a close and fruitful partnership with an advanced industrial nation; not through collectivization within a national framework, but through the inclusion of a progressively industrialized and decolonialized Tunisia in a much larger economic complex.

The continuation of the Algerian War, which none could have foreseen in the optimistic days following the independence of Tunisia and Morocco, forced the government to revise its earlier expectations, to give priority to political problems, and to cut some of its ties with France. Foreign private capital did not come forth as had been expected: on the contrary, European entrepreneurs and capital fled the country. American aid was insufficient to stimulate adequate economic growth. Above all, the Algerian War demanded a tightening of Tunisian nationalism, a faster tempo of political mobilization, a sense of urgency; the Bizerte crisis was the culmination of this trend.

Whereas economic planning was a divisive issue in 1956, in 1961 it appeared a useful instrument for strengthening national integration. New webs of solidarity and interdependence, as well as a sense of a common destiny, would be created through participation in the Ten-Year Plan. For the sake of success, sectional interests would give way to national discipline.

Whatever the correct interpretation of Tunisia's grand strategy, the creation of a tightly-woven national community took precedence over the goal of rapid economic expansion. The modern nation-state was to be built on civic virtues—and only afterward on economic accomplishments.

Perhaps this strategy of modernization—if such is the case—was based on a clear realization of the need to preserve at all costs Tunisia's main asset, its relatively cohesive society. This society shared some of the characteristics of the Western European states during the period of national awakening—in sharp contrast to most underdeveloped countries. Tunisia's assets were the existence of a state, well-defined boundaries, a common ethnic and language group, a large proportion of independent producers (particularly in the long-settled villages of the Sahel), a relatively well-developed system of transportation and communication, and, above all, a close-knit political elite.

This elite was large and homogeneous and cut across the various social strata. The long struggle for independence had made it one politically. And it had not had to face the determined opposition of the traditionalist elite, which had disintegrated under the impact of intensive colonialization.[6]

The new Tunisian elite largely lacked the entrepreneurial motivations present in Western Europe, but it showed the same concern with the elimination of privilege and arbitrary power, with the creation of a legal order guaranteeing basic freedoms and equality of opportunity, and with the need to bring about rapid economic growth. The values held by Bourguiba and his followers have made them, in fact, true interpreters of the French revolutionary tradition—including the convenient Jacobin mystique of the general will. The deep impact of French culture over several decades made the Western-trained intellectuals highly receptive to the political ideology of the moderate left. The Tunisian students at French universities, particularly during the turbulent 1930's, absorbed not only the ideals of the great emancipators, but an object lesson in the dangers of political extremism. The eventual success of the moderate left in France offered to Tunisia the promise of political reforms which would lead to independence, and prevented the search for a revolutionary model borrowed from another country. It also nourished the image of the "good France," ready to emancipate colonial peoples, as opposed to the unreasonable resistance of the "other France"—an image that has justified the tactics of Bourguibism. Perhaps this absorption of what amounts to a Radical Socialist ideology, generous in its intentions but fuzzy in its economic programs, can explain, at least in part, the absence of major economic reforms during the first four years following liberation.

The effort to maintain social cohesion—and the resulting caution in economic policy—was motivated not only by a desire to avoid a split within the political elite, which was not ready in 1956 and 1957 to accept the discipline, austerity, and dangers of collectivization, but also by the need to educate the masses, to convince them that modernization was both desirable and unassailable. Now that independence had been acquired, the concept of progress was to give a new and positive meaning to the ideal of freedom. With the active or passive support of large segments of the population, the government could embark upon the second phase of modernization with little danger of facing a strong, organized opposition, which the revolt of Ben Youssef had proved was always a possibility.

The education of the masses in a new perspective and a new civic morality implied a resolute attack on the strongholds of traditionalism, insofar as they clashed with the goals of modernization and the new democratic ethics. This attack risked shocking and embittering many people. Even the most popular leader could not afford to antagonize, at the same time, both traditionalists and conservatives. The most efficient strategy of change, fully compatible with the need to keep the people together, would involve a vigorous offensive against the traditionalists, coupled with a cautious and pragmatic economic policy that would not offend the conservatives.

The attack against tradition, however daring it may appear, was in fact relatively safe, given the discredit into which the traditional elite had fallen and the power of the party. The battle for modernization acquired a dramatic quality with the very daring of the government's offensive against such taboos as the religious fast of Ramadan. The shock treatment allowed a probing of the limits beyond which change would endanger the popularity of the government. It also gave the impression of a determined forward movement that would satisfy the more radical elements of the modernizing elite and impress the uneducated.

2. Social Change: Clearing the Way to Progress

In the Tunisian approach to modernization, a choice place has been given to the "psychological revolution," in the belief that it is necessary first to "transform attitudes," establish a "new scale of values," create a "revolutionary spirit." The frequent use of the words "mobilization," "attack," "campaign," and "war" in connection with routing prejudice, inertia, ignorance, and fatalism implies a concerted and all-out effort. This effort itself is based on the conviction that it is possible to transform attitudes, tear down the mental obstacles to progress, broaden horizons, and commit men to the fight for a better society.

The molding of the new Tunisia has involved the formation of both expectations and civic virtues. The people have been told that in ten years everyone will be decently housed, educated, and free from poverty. But they have also been told that persistence, discipline, and intelligence are needed for success. It is only if the Tunisian becomes a good citizen, capable of initiative, eager to learn and cooperate, that the battle against underdevelopment will be won. Not only a new morality, but a new sensitivity to wrongs must be created. The Tunisian people have to be taught to be shocked by situations they have long accepted passively. They have to be shamed out of their inertia and ignorance.

Their leader, who is in close and creative communication with his people, has made a point of instilling in them a new and revolutionary spirit. His message is direct, forceful, and easily comprehended. Philosophical principles and practical advice are poured forth in colorful and simple language. The frequent speeches are eagerly awaited and listened to over the blasting radios in the cafés and shops. They are commented upon. The message is amplified by the party in its role as educator.

The themes that he constantly reiterates reflect Bourguiba's deep faith in the perfectibility of man and in his own ability to mold his people in the image he has formed of the new Tunisia. As C. F. Gallagher has noted:

> One often feels that Habib Bourguiba is dealing with Tunisia by alternately prodding, scolding, envisioning, crying and decrying as a Pygmalion with four million Galateas. It is an enormous, unending personal effort to remake the character, thoughts, and habits of his countrymen to the image of his inner eye. In this there is much paternalism, more than a shade of vanity, and a whisper of the obsession of the true fanatic, without whom men would probably still be eating nuts and berries.[1]

Bourguiba's vision is essentially rational and realistic. National solidarity is not to be based on a negative and escapist formula of national self-assertion. As late as January 12, 1961, in a speech "Building a New Tunisia," he poked fun at those leaders of newly independent countries who keep raising the bogey of colonialism and neocolonialism:

> If progress is not made, they say it is because of the still-existing colonialism everywhere; from then on all failures are justified. . . . This mystique of a struggle to the end against imaginary enemies is accompanied by a similar mystique of endless victories. This is repeated to such a point that one begins to wonder why the battle continues in spite of so many victories. . . . The people can be abused by sterile struggles and imaginary success only for a certain time.

To this escapist formula he contrasts his own solution:

> We are in no need to feed people with illusions. Our prestige is due to the cohesion of the people and the efficacy of our methods. . . . We have built factories and houses, we have revived fallow land and dug wells. But before doing this we addressed the people. In order to channel their sentiments we appealed to reason and good sense. We exerted all efforts so that the people should grasp the importance of the struggle for economic prosperity.
>
> We have previously mobilized the people against colonialism. We persuaded them to revolt against the humiliation and the indignity of their condition. Once that battle was won, the struggle against misery

was yet to be fought. This was no easy matter and required a total reconversion of minds. The leaders—the responsible ones—the civil servants, the people, have all acquired a new awareness of the problem they are facing. . . . This consciousness explains the mobilization of Tunisian energies. It is not a mobilization directed against imaginary enemies, but rather toward constructive work, a rational organization of efforts, the application of programs of action, and a full exploitation of human possibilities and technical know-how. This is the secret of Tunisia's advance, the method by which we will rapidly reach the stage that all Tunisians hope for: a respectable position among the advanced countries.

And on June 26, 1961, he again stressed the means of accomplishing the psychological revolution, in a speech on "Neo-Destourian Socialism." Just as in the battle for independence "we spread the notions of dignity to the whole nation," now the same "driving force" must be used in the struggle against underdevelopment.

This is a hard task to accomplish, for it is not easy to inculcate in a man sentiments that are unknown to him. In the miserable state in which he vegetates, the poor fellow is not aware of the indignity of his situation. . . . We have to forge a new notion of dignity. In order for man to be more and more encouraged to raise himself above the level of an animal, he must understand the true meaning of his existence as a man. It is up to us to inculcate in him the notion of pride and respect for himself and others. . . . Thus we must in the economic sphere take up the propaganda we used against foreign domination and its humiliations.

He went on to say that the time had come to organize and coordinate all activities through the Plan, and that the people must participate in its orientation and choice of priorities.

Consenting to a limitation of liberty demands a profound mental transformation. A true psychological revolution is necessary in order to assure the success of the Plan once it is put into execution. So far we have been preparing peoples' minds. . . . A new conception of national solidarity is being born. . . . The struggle will not end in success unless there is full realization that what is at stake is human dignity, without which life is not worth living.

Thus, material progress is justified in terms of the highest moral values, and the methods to be used in terms of a lofty goal. The concepts of the dignity of the individual and of social solidarity are the motivating forces to help Tunisians accept willingly the limitation of their liberties, just as their energies were mobilized in the struggle for liberation. Humanistic ethics is the heavy artillery that will breach the fortresses of indifference, prejudice, and selfishness. Even religion is used to reinforce the new ideals. Thus the speech on Neo-Destourian socialism affirms that the companions of the Prophet

> . . . were socialists before the invention of the word, considering themselves members of the same family. They were not individualists; not one among them sought enrichment at the expense of the others. All worked for the common good. By turning back to the sources of Islam, we are to imitate them in their self-sacrifice, their love of their neighbors, and their sense of solidarity.

There are times, however, when the need to modernize clashes with some aspects of religion. On February 5, 1960, speaking of the fast of Ramadan, Bourguiba said, "It is inconceivable that religion can be an obstacle to the well-being and progress of the Moslems. It is unthinkable that it should become a factor in stagnation and weakness." Here the issue is met squarely, but precautions are taken to avoid the impression of a new morality clashing with the old. People are asked to "give up bad habits" and to "throw out the worst customs" in the name of a higher morality that the Prophet himself would have approved. The fast of Ramadan is "an abusive interpretation of the religion." Bourguiba reminded his listeners that the Prophet once told his friends, "Eat, eat, you will be stronger to meet the enemy": "Those are admirable words. We should comment on them at the Mosque on Friday; they are perfectly adapted to our situation. We have a great enemy to fight—Misery—and by the Prophet's voice God asked us to be stronger to conquer this enemy."

Bourguiba made it clear that he did not ask the people to give up the fast, "a commandment to be respected," unless it endangered health or interrupted necessary activities. Yet in saying this, he presented them with a dilemma which many resented, for to the Tunisian people Ramadan was the most concretely significant aspect of their religion, as well as a welcome break in a monotonous life. But the therapy of shock was partly successful; whatever the actual response to the arguments against fasting—' here the evidence is mixed—one more breach had been made in the fortress of traditionalism. The bluntness of the attack made a wide gap through which new ideas could penetrate.

Admonition and shock were not the only weapons in the strategy of psychological and social change. To be effective, the new set of values had to be demonstrated by deeds. The often spectacular transformation of living conditions through city planning, the tearing down of old houses, the building of new markets, schools, hospitals, and administrative buildings, and the creation of model villages were other tangible ways of transforming attitudes and mores. The thousands of workers in hundreds of work sites building terraces and ditches, widening roads, and planting trees give striking evidence of the government's determination to modernize. They are part of the campaign to change the minds of men. The heavily veiled Tunisian mother admiring the pristine new fish market just erected in her quarter is committed to modernization despite herself.

At the same time, some basic reforms were undertaken as early as 1956 to remove obstacles to progress: reform of the judicial system, emancipation of women, a major effort at universal education, and elimination of the *habous* system of landholding.*

* Some of these reforms involving changes in Islam were hard blows for the traditionalists. Thus the reform of Tunisian justice led to the retirement of many judges of the abolished Sharia courts. But as is typical of Bourguiba's style of governing the ground for the reform had been prepared by careful diplomacy. One of the leading religious figures, Tahar Ben Achour, was appointed rector of Zitouna University, while his son, Fadl Ben Achour, a distinguished scholar, was given an important post in the Ministry of Justice. In 1961, the son became rector of the new faculty of theology at the University of Tunis, and is today, as "Muphti de l'Etat," the leading religious authority in the country. The father retired after opposing Bourguiba's stand on the fast of Ramadan.

Religious opinion is, of course, dissatisfied with the reforms of the regime. But the protests are isolated and ineffective. The only serious incident, revealing organized mass protest, was the night-long riot that erupted in the city

The Emancipation of Women

The granting of independence to Tunisia accomplished in one stroke what thirty years of modernist evolution had been unable to achieve—the liberation of women. In 1956, the enactment of a modern domestic code, of Western inspiration, destroyed a stronghold of Islamic law and put the country ahead of all others in the Moslem world by establishing the legal framework for the total emancipation of women. Polygamy, unilateral repudiation, and forced marriage were abolished. At the same time, the principle of civic equality gave women the right to full citizenship.

These revolutionary steps had been prepared for by a slow evolution in mores, particularly among the educated urban groups. But it took the explosion of triumphant nationalism to brush aside ancient customs sacralized by Islamic law. The prestige of the liberator and of the victorious Neo-Destour had reduced the supporters of the Old Destour to sullen silence. The educated young generation was ready to accept gratefully from a Tunisian government what would have been bitterly resented had it come from the foreign ruler. Conditions were ripe to turn the political revolution into a social revolution by attacking the old society in its most sensitive area, the family structure.

The patriarchal family was the basis of the social structure. The absolute authority of the father gave him the right to arrange the marriage of his child-daughter. Once married, she was at the mercy of her husband. He could take other wives or concubines, and could repudiate her for no other reason than his desire to marry a more attractive woman and his inability to support two wives. This custom of "successive polygamy" was solidly entrenched in the lower strata of the urban population; true polygamy existed almost exclusively among the Bedouins, where several wives were a definite economic asset. When repudiated or divorced, a woman had to abandon her children, however young, to her husband's family and return to the authority of her own father. She herself had slight chance of obtaining redress of

---

of Kairouan, the citadel of religion and tradition, in mid-January, 1961. The occasion for the riot was the transfer of a popular schoolteacher because of his seditious sermons at Kairouan's oldest mosque.

legitimate grievances: the Sharia judge had little sympathy for a complaining woman.[2]

In the cities and villages, women and girls above the age of ten were usually kept within the house; if they did go out, they were heavily veiled. They were forbidden any form of social life or job opportunity, except as artisans in their homes. Although much better treated in the houses of the Sahel than in the tents of the hinterland, they were everywhere considered an inferior brand of human being, to be kept in fear and awe of their masters.

This family structure had hardly been dented by the impact of intensive nationalism and the zeal of reformists. In 1930, when Tahar Haddad wrote that the Koran had not imposed but merely tolerated practices that were no longer legitimate, that it should be reinterpreted in the spirit of the Prophet's true intentions, his book was immediately and solemnly condemned by the Zitouna Council. The prestige of the Great Mosque, strengthened by the French authorities, the forces of tradition, and the caution that the Neo-Destour had to exercise in the domain of religion, prevented any significant change of customs.

This situation retarded the economic growth of the country and was in direct contradiction to the humanistic and democratic values held by the modernists. It weighed on the conscience of the reformers, and perpetuated a feeling of inferiority toward the West. It had to be eliminated if the Tunisian people, both men and women, were to move quickly into the twentieth century.

Major changes in the institutions of marriage and divorce were introduced in the "Personal Status Code" of August 13, 1956, which replaced Koranic law with a unified legal system for all Tunisians—Moslems and Jews—placing them under the jurisdiction of common-law courts.[3]

Polygamy was prohibited. Although it affected probably less than 3 per cent of the population, mainly in the Center and the South, this prohibition was a daring step which no other Moslem state, with the exception of Turkey, has yet taken, for it opposes a literal interpretation of the Koran, which specifically recognizes the right of a believer to take four legitimate wives.

A similar disregard of rules sanctioned by religion appears in the legislation concerning marriage. Here again, the innovations are dictated by the principles of equality of the sexes and respect for human freedom and dignity. Article III of the Code transforms marriage from an agreement between two families to a contract based on the mutual consent of two individuals—without which the marriage can be annulled. The minimum age for marriage—eighteen for men and fifteen for women—prevents the widely practiced custom of the marriage of very young girls. When a young man reaches the age of twenty, he no longer needs the consent of his father or guardian to his choice of a partner. Even before this age he may appeal the dissent of his father before a judge—another significant blow at the patriarchal system.

Finally, religion is no longer an obstacle to marriage. Formerly, a Moslem woman could not marry outside her religion, although a man was permitted to wed a Christian or Jewish woman. Now Moslems of both sexes can marry without regard to religious affiliation.

On the subject of divorce, the new Code is characterized by the principle of the equality of the sexes and the necessity for judicial intervention. Unilateral repudiation, which kept wives in humiliating fear and dependence, is no longer possible. Divorce is based on mutual consent or on the initiative of one spouse; in either case, a judicial decision is needed, which may involve the payment of child support if the children remain with the mother. Compulsory intervention of the judge to determine the causes of the conflict and to attempt a reconciliation clashes with the traditional concern for complete privacy in family affairs. The lawmakers wisely assumed that fear of bringing conflicts into the open would keep divorces to a minimum.

The protection of children has been as great a concern of the Tunisian lawmaker as the protection of women and the liberation of the individual from the patriarchal family. New legislation has established rules for public as well as private guardianship of abandoned and vagrant children. The once familiar sight of children sleeping piled together on the sidewalks at night has been replaced by American-type "Boys' Towns," sheltering the "children of Bourguiba." Tunisia is the first Moslem country to introduce legal adoption, an institution which Islamic law ignored, thereby encouraging the selling or "renting" of children.

The legislation on succession favors the immediate family and increases the rights of female heirs—without, however, bringing complete equality. Here again the lawmakers have reduced the role of the patriarchal family and strengthened the solidarity of the immediate family, which is thought to be a more desirable and modern institution.

The new Code can be seen as an essential, but by no means sufficient, element in a strategy of social change. New principles, rules, and judicial procedures set a legal framework for accelerating an irreversible process of modernization. The Code was made possible by decades of slow evolution, and it, in turn, will facilitate further advances. But it does not pretend to take the place of other instruments for the transformation of attitudes and values. Education and job opportunities will translate the legal equality of women into reality; economic independence and intellectual accomplishments will buttress the guarantees of the Code and make them meaningful. Already thousands of women are employed in government and in industry and trade, and many more thousands are eager to acquire the skills that will give them freedom and equality.

The revolution in depth accomplished in Tunisia seems both more realistic and more solid than the radical secularization of Turkey, where, in attempting to outlaw old traditions, the government affected outward signs and symbols rather than underlying substance. In Tunisia, there is perhaps the same disregard for Islamic law, but not a formal rejection of the principles underlying it. The veil is indignantly condemned by Bourguiba as "a dust rag," but it is judged less important as a subject of legislation than the right of the husband to repudiate his wife in a moment of anger.

The results of the new legislation may not be spectacular. Except in Tunis and the larger cities, where many girls shed their veils the day of independence, the old custom of the veil has remained. Upon leaving high school, a girl returns to the veil, her home, and her father's authority. But chances are that she will have a voice in the choice of her husband and later in the raising of her children. Just as the illiterate mother accepted the revolutionary idea that her daughter should go to school, if only to attract a suitable husband, so the daughter will see that her own daughters do not hide themselves behind a veil. The two main reasons for its continued use—the opinion of elders and as a convenient *cache-misère,* an excuse for not buying expensive Western clothes—will by then have disappeared. The example set by Tunis, where the anonymity of a big city permits daring, will be followed elsewhere. The radio, the movies, and the television set will have prepared the ground. But the greatest instrument of liberation and equality remains the school.

The school has been the key to the door of modernization. Through it new mental processes, new ideas and values have accomplished a revolution in depth, whatever the survival of external signs of tradition. The speed of change is illustrated by the fact that 6,000 girls went to school in 1940, 70,000 in 1956, and almost 200,000 in 1961. The new Code is aimed at translating into law what the educated young generation already believes. Parents may for a time resist the process of change, but they cannot for long prevent new ideas from guiding their children's conduct. This is all the more so since the forebodings of traditionalists have not materialized. Observers have noticed the seriousness of purpose of the young generation and the absence of open rebellion. The law itself has seen to it that the young girl is adequately protected in her newly found freedom. A puritanical Code has increased penalties for loose morals. Not only illicit lovers but the best-intentioned ones are severely dealt with; elopement is punishable by two years in jail.*

The Educational Reform

The French cultural effort during the Protectorate had been far from negligible, and since 1945, the school enrollment has

* On the other hand, the legislator does not hesitate to antagonize religious or moral feelings when they conflict with the national interest, as was the case in 1961, when birth control was legalized, and the government suggested a limit of four children per family.

doubled every five years. But on the eve of independence, the number of Tunisian Moslems attending school was still less than one-third that of Tunisian Jews and of Europeans; in the university, less than one-tenth. Only one Tunisian child out of four attended primary school, and one out of thirty, secondary school.[4]

Under the ten-year education program launched in 1958, it is hoped that universal primary education will be achieved by 1969, and that one child out of three graduating from primary school will continue his education. Primary school attendance is expected to climb from 320,000 in 1958–59, to 836,000 in 1968–69, and the number of students in secondary schools and universities is expected to quadruple over this period. If the program is to be successful, 9,500 more teachers will be needed in primary schools, and 4,600 more in secondary and technical schools—that is, roughly three times the number of teachers in 1958. The annual cost of education is to triple in ten years; it was 17 per cent of the national budget in 1958–59, more than 20 per cent in 1960–61, and 25 per cent in 1961–62.[5] Of the total investment of the Three-Year Plan 1962–64, 11 per cent is earmarked for education.*

Obviously, a program of this magnitude is predicated upon the belief that Tunisia can quickly develop its economy, and upon faith in the soundness of a maximum investment in human resources. Whereas the principle of universal primary instruction is accepted as the obvious responsibility of a modern state, the

---

* According to the government's Ten-Year Perspective (*Perspective Décennale de Développement, 1962–1971*), the number of students in secondary schools will increase from 30,220 in 1961 to more than 115,000 in 1970. Of the 20,600 who will graduate by 1970, about 12,000 will enter universities. At the same time, 46,000 will graduate from intermediary schools to become white-collar and skilled workers.

Government statistics for the Three-Year Plan: 1962–1964 show that 79 per cent of all children aged six to seven were admitted to primary schools in 1961; 91 per cent will be admitted in 1963, and 97 per cent in 1965. About 3,300 additional teachers will be needed during the three-year period. Most of these will be Tunisians (only 750 foreign teachers will be retained), including 1,000 new teachers to be recruited each year from students who fail to graduate from secondary schools.

The figures given in the Perspective concerning the needs in teaching personnel during the 10-year period are: 8,527 teachers for primary schools, 915 for intermediate schools, and 4,537 for secondary schools.

expansion of secondary education is justified in terms of its effect on the economic future of Tunisia.

A publication of the Ministry of Education explains that secondary education is essentially to train "technical and non-technical cadres," and "must therefore be adapted to the economic and social needs of the nation." The ten-year program has deliberately eliminated the likelihood of a rural economy, which would have required that no more than 2 to 3 per cent of the total population receive a secondary education, as was the case in nineteenth-century France. The government bases its calculations on the expected rapid industrialization of Tunisia and on such a complete transformation of its economic and social structures as would rule out any fear of a surplus of highly trained personnel. "In a well-developed economy the jobs that do not require a high level of instruction and qualification tend to be less and less numerous, and those that require a very advanced level of general and technical training tend to be more and more numerous."[6] The real problem is to avoid an eventual shortage of technicians, which would slow down the economic development of the country.

The need to establish the human prerequisites for economic development is only one of the motives behind the ten-year program. The other is the need to create social and political integration by building up the cultural substructure needed by a modern nation-state. The new Tunisia needs a unified educational system through which the whole people can be transformed and molded in the image of its modernist elite.

In the past, Tunisian youth was educated under widely different educational systems. Those going to French schools hardly knew Arabic and were largely ignorant of Islamic culture, while the thousands trained in the Zitouna system were not fitted for positions in the modern sectors of the society. The dangerous cleavage between the modernists and the traditionalists was only partly bridged by Sadiki College and the Franco-Arab schools, with their combination of a modern curriculum and training in Arabic.

In 1947, Professor Mahmoud Messadi, who in 1958 was to become Minister of Education and the main author of the reform, put the claim to cultural unity clearly, in an article written for an Arabic-language review:

> It is a sacred principle of general pedagogy—the necessity of safeguarding the cultural unity of the country. This is a corollary of the idea that we developed earlier: education is social integration. If the society is a living reality, one and indivisible, then the culture will be so as well, and the pedagogical system must be a harmonious whole, with the task of preventing the unity of the whole from being placed in peril. To ignore the principle of cultural unity is . . . to sow the seeds of discord and . . . another unavoidable consequence . . . to place [the society] in peril of death.[7]

"The principle of cultural unity" implied, in fact, less safeguarding than creating. A common culture had to be shaped that would become the substructure for the "one and indivisible" nation-state, itself in the process of creation. The main obstacle to this was obviously traditionalism. The synthesis sought between Westernization and Tunisian Islamic culture had to be weighted in favor of the foreign import if modernization was to be effective. In other words, modernization had to take precedence over Tunisification.

It is characteristic of the Tunisian experience that during the first two years after independence nothing was changed in the existing system except the traditional Zitouna type of education. In April, 1956, the old annexes of Zitouna University were integrated into the secondary system of national education and the Mosque-University was made a public institution with a rector responsible to the Minister of Education. This was the prelude to the more radical measures taken in 1958. It was already obvious that the synthesis sought in the unified system would be at the expense of the traditional religious education held in contempt by the modernists.

This was to be expected. The attempts to bring fresh blood into the old Zitouna system had largely failed. Although the great Mosque-University had increased its student body some tenfold in the twenty years preceding independence, its prestige had steadily declined. Only the poorest students, frustrated intellectually and materially, continued to acquire there an education—Islamic law and literature and religious apologetics—that was of little practical value in an increasingly modern society. The low prestige of the old system and the fact that the ulema had generally been on the wrong side of the political fence permitted a daring surgical operation.

A highly centralized, uniform, pyramidal educational system in the best French tradition was set up. It included all schools at all levels, although Zitouna students were allowed to complete studies already undertaken. If France furnished the administrative model, Sadiki College furnished the cultural one. Tunisification has come to mean the adoption of a bilingual, if not bicultural, system that stresses modern disciplines, especially science and technology, leaving a minimum of time for the study of the national language and culture—Islamic literature, Arab history, the history and geography of the Maghreb. If at the primary-school level French and Arabic are taught in almost equal proportions, in secondary schools, Arabic is relegated to a subordinate position, taking less than one-third of the class hours. French is the sole vehicle for the acquisition of modern scientific knowledge. It is characteristic that as much time is devoted to the study of the French language and literature as to Arabic language and literature, and even more characteristic that three times as many hours are given to the study of Western philosophy than to the teaching of Islamic thought. Only one hour a week is set aside for instruction in religion and morals. At the secondary-school level, and even more at the university level, the synthesis involved in Tunisification means essentially the adoption of the French system, with the addition of enough Arabic culture to distinguish it from French education—although perhaps not enough to furnish the basis for a sense of cultural identity. Although the ultimate goal is total Arabization, no one has ventured to guess how long the transitional period will last.[8]

Once French had been selected as the main language for secondary and higher education, it had to be introduced at the bottom of the educational pyramid, the primary level. This has meant relying on French teachers and Tunisians trained in the

French educational system rather than on graduates of Zitouna University, whose qualifications were contested by the modernists. It has allowed for speed in educating a maximum number of children with no sacrifice of standards. Since the target of universal primary education within ten years was, and still is, far above Tunisia's ability to produce the 1,000 new teachers needed each year, massive French aid has become essential for a period of time and at all levels of education.

The unified pyramid system rules out a radical shortening of the program in primary schools, which the shortage of teachers would have justified. For lower standards in primary education would be reflected in secondary and later in higher education; the base of the educational pyramid has to be solid. Instead, a compromise between speed and quality has been found by cutting instruction down to fifteen hours a week during the first two years, and to twenty-five hours during the last four years, which allows for a considerable saving in teachers. Another solution has been found in cutting primary education from seven years to six.

At the secondary-school level, the dilemma of quality-quantity has a further dimension: the need to train large numbers of technicians and at the same time maintain a high level of general education. The goal of the reform is the rapid formation of the cadres needed for economic development at all levels: mechanics and draftsmen as well as engineers and scientists, office workers as well as administrators and managers. Secondary education must be adjusted to the need for both early specialization and the broad cultural background essential to future university students. One solution has been the creation of an intermediate three-year trade school side by side with the regular six-year secondary school. Students are directed to one or the other, according to ability, on the basis of a competitive examination given at the end of primary school. One graduate out of six enters these intermediate schools and one out of four the *lycées* or *collèges*.

The second solution is a polyvalent type of instruction in the regular secondary schools, aimed at forming both *cadres moyens* for trade and industry and future students for the universities; at striking a balance between general education and progressive specialization. After a first year of identical studies for all, the student is directed according to ability and tastes to one of three programs of studies: general, technical, and economic. Specialization is introduced slowly during the next two years, accompanied by a program of vocational guidance, and is intensified in the last three years. The general program offers concentration in Arabic, French, mathematics, and science; it also includes a subprogram for the training of future schoolteachers. The economic program leads to a terminal degree in bookkeeping or stenography or to higher economic and business studies at the university level. Similarly, the technical program leads either to the training of technicians for the various branches of industry or to entrance to an engineering school.

In 1958, school attendance varied considerably, from a high of 65 per cent in Tunis and 56 per cent in Sfax to a low of 17 per cent in a western governorate. The plans, however are to have a uniform proportion of primary schools for the number of school-age children throughout the country and to have each of the governorates build at least two large *lycées* and other *collèges* before the end of the ten-year period. This eminently democratic program corresponds to the concept of "education as social integration," the molding of a nation, "one and indivisible," whatever the cost involved.[9]

At the apex of the educational pyramid is the University of Tunis, officially created in March, 1960. Still consisting of scattered buildings throughout the city, it will shortly have its own beautiful campus two miles from the heart of Tunis. Now limited to 2,500 students—plus another 1,500 studying abroad, mainly in France—the University of Tunis will have about 12,000 students in 1970, including a sizable number of female students. The University has taken the place of the Institut des Hautes Etudes, which has been in existence in Tunis since 1945 and, under the sponsorship of the Sorbonne, has offered degrees in various disciplines at the level of the *licence*. Now Tunisian students can obtain Tunisian *licences* equivalent to French degrees for higher studies abroad.

In order to meet the requirements of modern higher education, the University will emphasize research, and it plans to have a number of research institutes, including one for the social sciences and another for nuclear physics. Zitouna has become merely a School of Theology and Religious Science in the new university. It is interesting to note that the School of Law is divided into three sections—law, economics, and business administration—a significant departure from the French model. It is also typical of the new Tunisia that more students are enrolled in the School of Science than in any other.

In the following statement, the Minister of Education made it quite clear that the source of inspiration for the new university will not come from the East:

> The example of certain young universities created in the last forty years in various countries formerly dependent or underdeveloped, notably in the countries of the Arab Near East, demonstrates that a university which is not sufficiently concerned with research rapidly becomes a teaching institution, the level of which approaches some sort of complementary secondary education.[10]

Three years after its inception, it seems clear that the goals set by the educational reform are largely being met on schedule, both quantitatively and qualitatively. Some localities are even ahead of schedule in raising the funds needed for building primary schools. Impressively modern *lycées* have been built in the poorest governorates. Tunisian teachers have been recruited in adequate numbers. Although many teachers lack sufficient training, the Ministry of Education claims, on the basis of reports of French and UNESCO inspectors, that the standards have been maintained. Vocational guidance has been a success from the beginning.[11] Even the Bizerte crisis did not prevent schools from operating normally, and most of the French teachers returned in October, 1961.

Popular response among the education-starved Tunisians has been encouraging. Illiterate parents are eager to send their children to school, and are bitterly disappointed when they fail the examinations to enter secondary school, knowing well that this is the avenue to a better life. Technical schools no longer need to recruit from the mediocre students who used to attend *faute de mieux;* now they cannot accept all qualified candidates.

The educational program seems to be the maximum effort compatible with existing and expected resources. It is elastic enough to lend itself to the requirements of economic planning; new educational targets can shift students from one field of specialization to another to fit expected job opportunities. The framework exists for an optimum use of human resources.

On the political side, the democratic quality of the educational system is a major asset. Equality of opportunity and vocational guidance give each child the chance to go up the educational ladder in the field of studies that suits him best. The new and considerably enlarged elite of tomorrow will be recruited on the broadest possible basis—an essential condition for social peace and political cohesion.

Aside from the possibility that the program may in the long run prove too ambitious, that quantity and speed will be obtained at the expense of quality, there are several dangers lurking beneath its very real merits. One is the other side of the coin of the rapid acquisition of knowledge and transformation of values: the creation of expectations that may not be fulfilled, particularly in the poorer regions. Even assuming that a fast-growing economy can absorb the graduates of the schools, many will have been eliminated halfway on the road to a degree; relatively harsh elimination may be necessary to maintain high standards. On the other hand, there is the eventual danger that a new proletariat will be formed with intellectual pretentions but no adequate skills.*

* The Ten-Year Perspective indicates that 60 to 70 per cent of the secondary school students will fail to graduate. A systematic effort is planned to provide for them. Those who fail during the last three years of schooling will be trained to become middle echelon technicians and primary school teachers. Those who fail during the first three years will be grouped with the drop-outs of intermediate schools to become industrial and white collar workers. This, the Perspective states, presents a certain risk of overproduction of semiskilled and skilled personnel. But it adds that "it is always good to provide the opportunity for the greatest number of citizens to be raised be-

Another problem stems from the bilingual aspect of the program. Will it encourage an integrated individual, or create a certain ambivalence among people who will wonder about their Tunisian identity? This ambivalence may have unforeseen social and political consequences in shaping the character of Tunisian nationalism. Although today's busy Sadiki graduate seems to take in stride his mixed cultural background, a show of extreme confidence may well betray an inner lack of sureness.

Another side of the bilingual problem is its implication of a continued dependence on France. Until the Bizerte crisis, this cultural dependence had not troubled the Tunisian modernists. They had accepted with a certain amount of pride the fact that by selecting French as the language of secondary instruction, they had chosen to remain within the French cultural orbit, with all its special idiosyncrasies. Observers have noticed what amounts in fact to a provincial cultural outlook, despite vigorous claims to cosmopolitan universality. In practical terms, this dependence derives from the need to imitate French methods and curricula, if only to assure degree equivalence for students who seek higher degrees at French universities or *grandes écoles*. But dependence has meant, above all, the need for French teachers at all levels of education, a need which will remain for the next few years. Recruiting native Tunisian teachers at the primary and secondary level cannot be speeded up without sacrificing other vital sectors and the very success of economic development. At best, it is a long-term undertaking, and the present selection of from 20 to 30 per cent of the secondary school students for teacher training seems an absolute maximum. Even at this rate, self-sufficiency will not be obtained for another six to eight years.

In retrospect, it seems clear that the reform program of 1958 meant that the goal of modernization, implying continued dependence on France, had priority over the goal of Tunisification. The implications of the choice made in 1958 became brutally

yond primary school level and intellectual investment at all levels and good vocational training . . . are the most effective means of raising the general standards of a nation."12

evident in 1961 during the Bizerte crisis. It is probable that one of the main reasons for the compromise reached in September was the government's need for the services of some 3,000 French teachers. On the other hand, it would be difficult now to ignore the lesson of Bizerte and pretend that educational reform need not be adjusted to the claims of a self-assertive nationalism. The search for greater cultural independence may well lead either to speeding up the process of Arabization, or to a more cosmopolitan approach, with the introduction of a third language as an alternate means for acquiring modern knowledge.

Reforms in Land Tenure

In his book *La Tunisie d'Aujourd'hui et de Demain,* Gabriel Ardant notices that the obstacles facing twentieth-century Tunisia on its road to progress are basically not different from those that faced French reformers two centuries earlier. At first, these reformers concentrated on problems concerned essentially with individual and property rights. These were also the first preoccupation of the Tunisian Government. The suppression of the *habous* was thus "the equivalent of the secularization of the Church properties and of the abolition of certain archaic land structures realized in France in 1791."[13]

At independence, the *habous* lands totaled about 4 million acres, or one-fourth of the arable land of Tunisia. Some *habous* covered huge areas, others an acre or less, since owners of a parcel of land often held in reserve a *habous* title to their property. Originally, the custom had grown out of the need to protect family property from the risk of confiscation and excessive division among heirs; despite its pious justification, it was more often than not a convenient system to bypass the rights of female inheritors.

A huge mortmain patrimony had thus been established, covering at one time as much as 40 per cent of the arable land. Although justified in the past by public insecurity, the *habous* had come to constitute an anachronism that was a major obstacle to rational use of the land. The administrator—nominated by the *caïd* when too many beneficiaries were involved—had no incentive to invest in the land, nor had the thousands of "tenants," who were often seminomadic squatters without any guarantee of tenure. The system had a paralyzing effect on agricultural improvement.[14]

French initiative in land registration—which has been described in Part I of this book—had led to a substantial improvement in the traditional land tenure and prepared the ground for the elimination of a system that had lost its *raison d'être*. Most of the public *habous* land suitable for colonization had in fact been appropriated by the end of the Protectorate. But the private *habous* were a more difficult problem, because of the large numbers of beneficiaries and the insistence of Islamic law that the consent of each beneficiary had to be obtained before any change in the status of the property could be made. The rights of the beneficiaries conflicted with those of the tenants, putting the French administration in a quandary when it attempted to protect the latter. The number of private *habous* had in fact increased substantially during the French occupation as a device for protecting Moslem families from land-hungry colonizers. The French inroads against the traditional system were bitterly resented and had been condemned by the early nationalist movement.

Yet the problem of maximum use of land resources was the most pressing one in a country whose small industry was unable to absorb the excess rural population, including some 200,000 unemployed. The modern values of economic efficiency and social justice condemned the archaic system of land tenure. The problem was no longer, as it was in the early days of the French occupation, to find vigorous entrepreneurs to whom virgin land could be handed over, but to distribute undercultivated land as equitably as possible among as many laborers as possible. Since the distribution of the properties owned by the *colons* would have been not only inadequate but economically disastrous, *habous* land offered the most promising opportunity to relieve the worst consequences of underproduction and overpopulation.

During the occupation, the Neo-Destour could not make an issue of the *habous* system—any more than it could attack another traditionalist stronghold, the Zitouna system of education. After the liberation there was no reason to hesitate. The inefficiency of the *habous* was not the only factor involved. Much of the private *habous* land was owned by the "old turbans," traditionalist families of the upper bourgeoisie who had been the supporters of the Old Destour. Now the opportunity came to humble opponents of the Neo-Destour while eradicating an institution that prevented economic progress. Thus the logic of enlightenment and social justice, the desire for economic efficiency, and political considerations were all combined in condemning a major obstacle to progress and a symbol of archaism. In the political climate of independence, this was an aspect of modernization that could be embarked upon safely and with a good conscience. The fact that the suppression of the *habous* encouraged private property rather than collective farming scandalized only a few Tunisians.

A decree of March 2, 1956, transferred to the state all public *habous* property. This was justified by the fact that the state now administered all cultural and charitable services formerly performed by religious bodies. The law involved some 325,000 acres, which became part of the public domain. Of this, some 150,000 acres still remained in 1961, the rest having been distributed, sold, or given to individuals through the governors and the Neo-Destour political commissioners—a useful source of political patronage. In addition, the domain also acquired some 800,000 olive trees (fruit trees being measured in number of trees rather than in acreage), two-thirds of which have been sold or given away.

The abolition of private *habous* was realized by the law of July 18, 1957, which established a procedure for the distribution of land based largely on equity. Administration commissions have attempted to satisfy the rights of both beneficiaries and traditional occupants. The law has both economic and social advantages: not only do property titles open access to credit and encourage initiative and hard work, but large *habous* lands are distributed among hundreds of new owners.

This represents a huge and lengthy effort. After the preliminary topographical work come long inquiries and the litigation of conflicting claims. Originally, regional commissions under the governors were to handle the liquidation of the *habous* in each governorate. There were so many appeals to the "Cour de Cassation," however, that in 1960 the national assembly established a special tribunal to settle disputes more quickly; the tribunal decided some 1,000 cases in its first year, with 5,000 more still on its docket.

Another major initiative of the government is the distribution of collective tribal lands, which cover almost all the steppe-like territory south of Kairouan—5.5 million acres, half of which are arable. To this must be added 2.2 million acres of *"terres d'extrême indivision,"* former tribal land that has been divided among families without any consideration of property titles. Thus, more than one-half of the arable Tunisian territory was under a tenure system that prevented a rational use of land. A relatively dense, seminomadic population lived on these tribal lands; many were unemployed or underemployed. In rainy years, they would scratch the ground to obtain a meager crop, and the rest of the time they ranged far and wide to support themselves and their herds. For some decades, the trend had been toward individual appropriation of tribal land for purposes of cultivation, and two statutes, of 1918 and 1935, permitted the individual ownership of collective land. But the procedure was extremely slow and often not applicable, for the most enterprising members of the tribe had already carved out for themselves the choice parcels, in a completely anarchistic manner and without property titles. Yet the trend needed to be encouraged in order to facilitate a more rational exploitation of the land, particularly through the cultivation of olive and fruit trees.

After liberation, some people, including the Minister of Agriculture at the time, objected to the division of tribal land into small, ineffectual parcels and preferred to use the existing collective structure to establish large units in the style of the Russian kolkhoz. Others argued that collectivization was already out of the question, since individual appropriation was a *fait accompli,* demonstrating the individual spirit of the Bedouin. They further argued that the Bedouin's anarchistic tendencies could be controlled and corrected by the establishment of co-operatives of production. This solution was adopted, and the law of September 28, 1957, allows for the distribution of arable land to individual owners. This is done on the basis of present occupancy, with compensation to the tribe by the holders of the larger parcels. A chain reaction is expected to take place: Titles of ownership will mean easy access to credit and increase the incentive for optimum use of the land; at the same time, more intensive cultivation will allow more people to find jobs. The re-distribution of land in newly irrigated zones—*cellules de mise en valeur*—also offers the possibility of resettling large numbers of agricultural laborers, each owning a small lot—an experiment which so far has met with varying degrees of success.

The distribution of tribal land has proceeded at a speed ten times greater than during the French Protectorate, and a simpli-fication of procedures ought further to facilitate the process. It is a formidable undertaking, since it involves topographical surveys and cadastration of roughly half the Tunisian territory, and it is complicated by the fact that *de facto* ownership must often be denied and land redistributed to fit the requirements of rational exploitation.

Under the French Protectorate, the cadastre system—a survey of the land and delimitation of the property after rigorous examination of all claims and arbitration—had covered most of the north of the country. But it was a long and expensive procedure for establishing property deeds. In 1959, with the establishment of the Banque Nationale Agricole, a simple proce-dure was instituted: Credit was given to those who acquired certificates of possession from regional authorities. If after one month a claim was not challenged, credit was granted. After a slow start, the process gained momentum, as the fellah realized he could get credit by getting a certificate of possession.

As for the *colon* lands, totaling 1.5 million acres, more than one-half had already been appropriated by the Tunisian Government in one form or another by the end of 1961—some through agreement and others through expropriation and sequestration. Originally administered by the governors, some of whom had not proved particularly efficient, the former *colon* lands are now under the jurisdiction of the Office des Domaines. Cooperatives of production have been started and more are to come, but much of the land will be leased in whole units to enterprising farmers for four-year periods—another victory for the partisans of private ownership, or perhaps an expedient dictated by the scope of the problems presented by collectivization.

The first genuine agrarian reform—as distinguished from reforms affecting the ownership of land—was taken by the law of June 11, 1958. In concerned the lower Medjerda Valley in northern Tunisia, a rich but marshy agricultural area of about 740,000 acres, on which the state, with French and later American aid, had spent millions of dollars in waterworks, thus increasing the value of the land two to four times. Since the land in the valley was distributed most unevenly, the law decided that the contribution of each proprietor to the "plus value" resulting from irrigation was to be in proportion to the size of his holding. Whereas owners of less than five acres were exempt from any contribution, the contribution of the large holder consisted in giving up part of his land. This land was distributed so that except under certain conditions no one was to own more than fourteen or less than five acres. To the concept of the equitable distribution of land was added the concept of its rational use: Owners would be penalized for not using their land to the optimum or for failing to convert to irrigated cultivation. The idea of social justice was thus combined with the idea of social function, to give the state the right to force a private owner to extract a maximum from his land.[15]

Private initiative, the concept of private property limited by the imperatives of social justice, and the need for maximum production seem to have guided the lawmakers in all early reforms concerning the status of land. It remains to be seen whether land redistribution will allow for both maximum productivity and the elimination of unemployment. The legal reforms, however essential a basis for agricultural development, are only one of its preconditions. Others involve such things as adequate facilities and, especially, the education of the farmer. This the Tunisian Government has fully realized. The new Banque Nationale Agricole is to make its loans conditional upon the willingness of the borrower to accept its technical directives: Credit and education will develop side by side and buttress each other. Similarly, the creation of experimental farms and the training of agricultural engineers and counselors will give efficacy to the new legal framework.

In the meantime, the multiplication of peasant proprietors is a factor of social cohesion. It is just as important in building up the new nation-state as equality of individual rights, universal primary education, and the widening of an elite recruited on democratic principles.

On June 11, 1961, a ceremony was held in the lower Medjerda Valley to celebrate the third anniversary of the promulgation of the law on agrarian reform. The property titles for 330 agricultural holdings were to be handed over to new settlers. This was the occasion for a typical and revealing Bourguibist performance.

The President explained in his speech that he had come to see for himself how the law was being carried out, how the people lived, and what they thought. After praising the work of the Managing Director of the Medjerda Valley Development and of his fellow workers, Bourguiba cited a few figures: fruit-production, which amounted to 550 tons in 1961, would be 630,000 tons in 1970; milk-production would be increased from 1,100 to 57,000 gallons. He then explained that a controlling and directing body was necessary, since most farmers did not have sufficient technical training to understand their true long-term interests.

Let us remember the manner in which the peasants kept their affairs secret and the secrecy with which they surrounded any borrowing transaction, as though it were a shameful act.

Good heavens! Why should seeking a loan for developing one's land and thus benefiting the farmer himself and the national interest be a dishonor?

But once the bank or state agency has made a loan it is only natural that it should also advise the recipient of the loan. If, by bad management, the farmer jeopardizes his own affairs and the yield of his land, he will not be the sole loser. The whole nation will lose with him. We are all bound together. Thus the concept of socialism takes on its full meaning.

In this republic of 4 million people, how can we leave family units, which are states in miniature ruled by autonomous chieftains, to fend for themselves? The state, which sees beyond the individual, must intervene for the sake of national solidarity.

Modern life cannot possibly allow unlimited freedom. The idea of absolute ownership, which leads to abusive administration, has had its day.

. . . Man is no longer free to dispose of his goods, whether they be land, factories, rent or salaries, regardless of reason, experience, or technology.

This is the philosophy and the basis of what one can call Neo-Destour Socialism. Socialism has been too often submerged by verbal propaganda and deception. As for ourselves, it is by using reason in the general interest that we have come to what we call socialism. This general interest is our constant guide.

Collective interest, he went on to say, could not be sacrificed to selfish individual interest. Profiteering would not be allowed. Speaking at some length of the meat speculators who took advantage of each drought, he said that the government would not hesitate "to strike at these wretched individuals." He continued:

You see that . . . we are now talking of the problems of meat and the schemes of speculators. Everything is interrelated; national solidarity implies arbitration by the state, which is responsible for social harmony. Reason dictates this role to the state. That is why I am addressing you in the name of reason, which is shared equally by all. As a member of the Tunisian community, I am explaining my view of what I think to be in your interest. What we need is not to practice a fierce individualism in the name of liberty, but to develop the idea of solidarity and socialism.

In order to succeed in this, those holding positions of responsibility in the government must be disinterested, of high moral standing, clearsighted and competent and, when necessary, they must be severe. At first, they must try argument and the force of persuasion. They must put advisers and guides at the disposal of citizens. When necessary, they must check tendencies towards insubordination.

. . . .

. . . Of course, the behavior and awareness of the citizen vary with his intellectual level.

This is why I have always said that the principal cause of underdevelopment was intellectual backwardness and an ignorance of moral values. We have tackled this backwardness with our ten-year program of schooling. . . .

Thus, all our problems are related. Our success in the economic and social struggle will depend on our moral and intellectual level. I address you constantly in order to help bring about this intellectual and moral improvement. I spare neither my time nor my health. As you all know, my vocal cords get so strained that I have to go abroad for treatment every year because of them.

It is comforting for me to watch the nation progress rapidly: profound revolutions, new ways of thought, a better scale of values, are all aspects of this miraculous rebirth of the Tunisian nation. We have resorted to neither a military nor a police state nor to any other repressive measures.

Through direct contacts, our citizens have been able to grasp the significance, the scope, and the aims of this government's initiatives, which are firmly supported by the party and national organizations.

This freely accepted discipline, this enthusiasm and the applause with which you welcome our suggestions, as well as the atmosphere of reason and mutual respect, form the essential basis of our regime. . . .

This speech reveals the talent of a leader who knows how to communicate his philosophy in a direct and concrete way. The most ignorant and meat-starved listener could understand and approve "Neo-Destour socialism." For him, the meat in his couscous warranted limitations on individual freedom. For the more sophisticated Tunisian, the President's call to "progress while respecting the freedom and dignity of the individual" could hardly be objectionable.

3. Economic Change:
From Pragmatism to Plan

At the time of independence, Tunisia inherited from the Protectorate a marked economic imbalance: a large traditional sector of subsistence, nonmarket economy side by side with a small, modern sector, predominantly in the north of the country.

The traditional sector—hardly changed from the Middle Ages —engaged 75 per cent of the population but produced less than one-fourth of the national income. It consisted mainly of low-yielding agriculture, animal husbandry, and handicrafts. Tens of thousands of artisans continued to make a meager living, in a protracted and losing battle against mass industry. The traditional farmers produced less than one-third as much wheat per acre as did those on modern holdings, and especially in central and southern Tunisia, they were at the mercy of droughts that frequently ruined crops and decimated the herds. Except in some areas along the coast, where fruit and olive trees had multiplied, conditions had deteriorated in the past forty years, population increasing faster than production. For the population as a whole, the per capita income was about $120 a year; in fact, it was only half as much for the majority of the rural population, especially in the southern and western parts of the country. There were hundreds of thousands unemployed and underemployed in the countryside despite mass emigration to the cities.

The modern sector included mainly large-scale production of cereals and wine grapes and a few modern plantations of olive and fruit trees. Approximately 1,000 Europeans and Tunisians in the modern sector owned one-third as much land as the half million small farmers in the traditional sector. Besides agriculture and trade, the modern sector included the mining of phosphates, iron, lead, and zinc, the production of which had declined over the last two decades, and some light industry, which had been given an impetus during and immediately after World War II. Industry—including mining—employed 9 per cent of the active population and accounted for less than one-fifth of the gross domestic product (GDP). Very few Tunisians had participated in the country's industrial development: of the 304 enterprises with more than 50 employees, only 30 were in Tunisian hands.[1]

Almost all growth in the Tunisian economy before World War II had been in the modern sector, which benefited from good roads and railroads, especially in the North. After the war, when the first stages of economic reconstruction were completed in France, large amounts of French capital, both public and private, were invested in Tunisia. In the public sector, the French Government undertook a program, called the Modernization and Equipment Plan, for rebuilding and expanding the infrastructure. A large part of this program provided for the development and equipping of railways, harbors, utilities, and a number of large dam and irrigation projects, including the Medjerda Valley Development.

With the agitation for independence, French private investment quickly slowed down, and with independence a large part of the European population, and thus a considerable amount of private capital, left Tunisia. By the end of 1960, only half of the European population, or about 100,000 people, remained. Furthermore, in 1957, the French Government cut off economic assistance because of Tunisian support of the Algerian rebel government. As a result, gross investment declined from 20 per cent of the GDP in 1950, to 10 per cent in 1958. The average annual rate of economic growth fell from 5 to 6 per cent for the period 1950–53 to 2 to 3 per cent for the period 1954–59. With an annual population growth rate of over 2 per cent, there was little or no growth in per capita income.[2]

Two developments largely prevented a complete deterioration of the Tunisian economy: excellent harvests in 1958 and 1959, and the signing, in March, 1957, of an economic and technical assistance agreement between Tunisia and the United States, which was to provide increasing amounts of aid each year. These developments were fortunate, for there was no systematic effort at development during the years following independence, but rather an empirical approach predicated upon Tunisia's ability to attract foreign and domestic capital and to produce a crop of managerial talent. But even favorable legislation on credit and tax advantages failed to bring about a substantial increase in private investment, particularly in industry. Bourguiba's repeated admonitions about the need for initiative and risk-taking met with little response; owners of capital preferred safe investment in land or a quick profit in trade.* The government's encouragement of private initiative through various incentives had to give way to more active intervention and to government participation in the creation of new business ventures.

By raising the problem of choice and priorities, this active intervention paved the way for the acceptance of the concept of state planning. As Bourguiba said when he introduced the idea of the Ten-Year Plan, on January 12, 1961:

> Any proposal for new enterprises, the creation of a cannery or a shoe factory, that a government agency chooses to present to me, might well be excellent. But how am I to judge the timeliness of the new undertaking, predict the progress . . . establish an order of priority in the setting up of enterprises? In this web of problems how can I consent to go forward gropingly, overlooking the questions which arise relative to the repercussions that each measure might have. . . .

The Plan thus appeared not as an ideological choice, but as the consequence of the state's assumption of functions that private initiative had failed to perform. Until that failure had been demonstrated, the government had preferred cautious experimentation to embarking upon a course of action for which it was unprepared technically and, perhaps, politically. During the two periods that can be discerned before the launching of the Plan

---

* Output in a number of industries, however, continued to rise after 1956. Production of electricity rose from 228 million kilowatt hours to 282 million kilowatt hours in 1961, a gain of almost 24 per cent. Construction increased by more than 100 per cent. Cement production increased from 360,000 metric tons in 1956 to 405,000 tons in 1960. Total deposits of the commercial banking system rose by 64 per cent and credits extended to the private sector by 44 per cent during the years 1959 and 1960.

in 1961, the emphasis was on stability rather than on thorough-going reform of structures.

Consolidation of Independence, 1956–59

Moving from protectorate or colonial status to independence requires judicious action if the resulting economic dislocations are to be minimized. The attainment of economic independence presented Tunisia with tremendous problems because of its varied and complex ties with France. The Tunisians undertook a skillful disengagement which satisfied their immediate needs for economic and political sovereignty, while preserving many economic ties with France.

With the advent of independence, there was a sharp decline in economic activity as a result of the departure of many French skilled workers, entrepreneurs, and owners of capital, and a wait-and-see attitude among those who remained. The Tunisian Government did succeed, however, in establishing economic stability in a very short time. Prices remained fairly stable; foreign exchange reserves were built up; the international value of the dinar was maintained; the operating budget of the government was brought into balance; and two development banks, one for industry and one for agriculture, were founded with the support of the government.

Good harvests and timely United States economic assistance contributed substantially to maintaining economic stability; however, the competence of the Tunisian Government, and its pragmatic approach in negotiating postindependence economic relations, especially with France, played a very large part.

Before independence, a customs union existed between Tunisia and France, allowing free entry of goods; foreign trade was therefore predominantly with France. Tunisia was a member of the franc zone, and used the centralized franc-area currency pool for its foreign exchange requirements. After independence, the Tunisian Government established the Central Bank of Tunisia and introduced the national currency unit, the dinar (today valued at U.S. $2.38), in November, 1958; it also initiated negotiations with the French to abrogate the customs unions, introduced an independent tariff system, and concluded a Financial and Trade Agreement with France in September, 1959. In short, the Tunisians succeeded in gaining control of their foreign trade and exchange and at the same time in establishing marketing arrangements with France for two key exportable surpluses—wine and durum wheat—at very favorable prices.

The record is equally good concerning public finance. The operative budget, which during the Protectorate was supported by the French Treasury, increased by almost 25 per cent between 1955 and 1960. Yet the government succeeded in balancing it, and even produced a small surplus. As for the investment budget, which depended upon French low-interest loans, it has been financed since 1957 from noninflationary sources, including U.S. economic assistance. In 1960, Tunisia's national debt was less than 5 per cent of the GDP, a good demonstration of the soundness of its public finance position.[3]

Between 1950 and 1957, Tunisia's foreign-trade deficit averaged over $50 million per year; it was covered by large French Government expenditures for its civil and military services and by an inflow of French capital. After independence, Tunisia's trade deficit was substantially reduced, averaging only $11 million per year for the period 1957 through 1959. This was due both to bumper crops and to the decline in economic activity that kept import levels stable. At the same time, strict controls over capital transfers to France removed one of the major drains on Tunisia's franc holdings. The combination of French Government expenditure—amounting to $36 million in 1959—and increasing U.S. assistance enabled Tunisia to build up its foreign-exchange reserves. At the end of 1959, total gold and foreign-exchange holdings amounted to $87 million, corresponding to approximately the value of seven months of imports at the 1959 rate.[4]

In summary, during the first three years of independence, the Tunisian Government pursued very conservative monetary and fiscal policies. At an African bankers' conference in the fall of 1960, which commemorated the second anniversary of the Central Bank of Tunisia, Hedi Nouira, the Governor of the Central Bank and a close adviser to Bourguiba, reviewed the economic development of the first three years of independence and stated that it had been the express policy of the Tunisian Government to build up its foreign-exchange reserves, protect the international value of the national currency, and maintain domestic price stability—all of which was no mean accomplishment for a new nation. In answer to critics of the government's conservative policies, Nouira added that stability was not an end in itself but a precondition for economic growth.[5]

Tunisia, having assured its economic independence, prepared to confront the problem of providing employment for its people and of initiating long-term economic growth.

The Battle Against Unemployment: 1959–61

The economic condition of the majority of the population was largely unchanged after three years of independence. The major problem, which had been chronic during the Protectorate, was the large number of unemployed and underemployed; numbering between 200,000 and 250,000, they made up about one-fourth of the male labor force.

As early as 1956, the government had attempted to fight unemployment—but in an unsystematic way. It soon succeeded in eliminating mendicancy and vagrancy. Abandoned children became "les enfants de Bourguiba" or were trained in trade schools. The Union Nationale des Femmes Tunisiennes (UNFT) enrolled hundreds of young girls and women to knit sweaters and make dresses for the National Vestiary. Older people were placed in institutions for the aged, while many younger men were given odd jobs as licensed car wardens and messenger boys. Efforts were made to revive and reorganize artisanal production, which fed perhaps as many as 100,000 people and gave a useful complementary income to many more. But in the absence of a fast-developing industry, the problem of unemployment was becoming more acute each year, particularly in Tunis, where thousands continued to flock from the southern and western provinces.

In the autumn of 1959, President Bourguiba toured the

country and repeatedly commented on the idleness and resulting degradation of jobless people. In one of his weekly speeches, on December 10, 1959, he said:

> We want all citizens to be imbued with the will to conquer misery and resignation, to uproot the belief in blind determinism. . . . The greatest problem is to engage the vast numbers of unemployed in the struggle against underdevelopment. The unemployed are capital that is asleep. This manpower can create wealth . . . and contribute to the national income.

The President then initiated the so-called "battle against underdevelopment and unemployment," saying that he would turn Tunisia into a vast work site.

Actually, the program of mobilizing the human resources of the country for economic development had begun in 1957 when, as the result of a drought, starvation and massive unemployment prevailed. The United States Government provided 45,000 tons of wheat, which were used for wage payments to needy persons on local work projects. In 1958, a new program was undertaken to meet the economic emergency that arose as a result of the departure of foreign capital and technicians. Wheat provided by the United States was used as payment in kind—supplementing a small cash wage supplied by the Tunisian Government—on economic development projects throughout the country. Some 75,000 were thus employed on a part-time basis. Here in effect was the first United States "Food for Peace" program.

In 1959, the government of Tunisia decided to expand the program, changing employment from part-time to full-time. The number of workers increased to 140,000. Work leaders called *animateurs* were trained and assigned to the work sites to instruct workers, ensure that work norms were met, and carry on an educational program. The daily wage consisted of three pounds of semolina and 200 millimes in cash supplied by the Tunisian Government, making a total equivalent to $0.67. (This is comparable to the basic agricultural wage of 350 millimes [$0.84] per day.) The program was continued and expanded, and the average number of workers increased to 160,000 in 1960 and to 210,000 in 1962.[6]

The program is planned by an administrator in the Ministry of Plan and Finance, but the priorities and actual operations are directed by the provincial governors and their deputies, with the assistance of the technical field staffs of such national ministries as Agriculture and Public Works. Most of the projects are concerned with land development and clearance, reforestation, terracing, road construction, drainage, and well and cistern construction, and are directly contributing to the country's economic development. A start has been made in training more workers in basic masonry and carpentry in order to use them in a nation-wide low-cost housing program.

This battle against underdevelopment demonstrates the imaginativeness and administrative ability of the Tunisian Government. The country's greatest resource, manpower, which historically has also been its greatest social and economic problem, in the form of widespread unemployment, was put to use in an economic development program in the shortest possible time and with a minimum of investment.

The economic accomplishments to date are impressive and visible to the most casual tourist, who is struck by the industry of the workers he meets at hundreds of work sites throughout the country. But of equal importance is the immeasurable effect the program has had on national morale. It has given the Tunisians pride in the tangible collective accomplishments that directly serve their own communities. Not only is the countryside being transformed, but the men bringing about this transformation have lost the opprobrium of being unemployed—a term frowned upon by Tunisian officials when applied to the men on the work sites. It has helped to reintegrate in rural communities people who had migrated to the cities in vain search of work. Finally, it has encouraged self-help projects and local planning, a precondition for the success of the long-term national Plan. The Tunisian program is now being adopted in many underdeveloped countries as an effective self-help measure, making use of U.S.

agricultural surplus commodities in labor-intensive investment projects.

Planning: The Ten-Year Perspective, 1962–71

Early in 1961, President Bourguiba announced the "year of the Plan"; the Tunisian Government would undertake a long-range program of economic and social development. The Office of the Plan was combined with the Ministry of Finance to form a super Ministry of Plan and Finance, which was placed under the direction of Ahmed Ben Salah. The Planning Section of the Ministry was reorganized and staffed with the best technicians available from all branches of the government. A series of studies was initiated in order to collect and analyze the data necessary for the preparation of the Plan, which was scheduled for release in the summer of 1961. The government made a major effort to educate the people about the purpose and methods of the Plan. Officials toured the country addressing mass audiences and consulting professional organizations. The Plan became the predominant theme of the President's weekly speeches.

"The time has come," he said on June 24, 1961, "to put order into all our activities and submit them to the discipline of reason." Private enterprise alone, he explained, could not bring about higher living standards, except slowly and at unnecessarily high cost. Only a collective effort could be efficient. "Individual efforts are uncoordinated. By being divergent they risk canceling each other out and even being harmful. While collective effort, on the contrary, if harmoniously conducted and led, is as efficient as a military operation. . . ." Planning was needed, he added, not only to coordinate efforts but to reserve an important part of the national income for productive investment and to direct savings into proper channels. Tunisians had to rely on themselves before relying on others. Discipline was essential; it was not, however, to be obtained through coercion, but through persuasion and full cooperation. People would not only accept the necessary limitations to their liberty, they would actively participate in the elaboration and execution of the program—

which was to be a "popular plan," a condition necessary for its success.

On August 23, 1961, President Bourguiba was presented with a *Perspective Décennale de Développement 1962–1971*, a Ten-Year Perspective for Economic Development, which, it was made clear, was not a plan but merely a "perspective" to be discussed and analyzed at the various levels of the government. By the end of 1961, the first stage, a Three-Year Plan for 1962–64, was to be ready for implementation. The introduction of the Perspective made it clear that the Plan is not based on any ideology or economic doctrine, but reflects the personality of the Tunisian people and the social and economic imperatives of the country. It embodies a "Tunisian type of socialism," which strives for cooperation and collective effort. Private enterprise has a place in the Tunisian economy, but it will be made to operate within the framework of the Plan. The introduction also states that the Plan is not to be a dictum, but will be flexible and responsive to the needs of the people.

The Perspective lists the general obstacles to economic development, from meager natural resources and irregular rainfall to a lack of trained personnel and sufficient investment capital, due to the low level of domestic savings. It pinpoints the smallness of the domestic market and the vulnerability of Tunisia's foreign exchange earnings, which depend on prices established in international markets for Tunisia's principal exports. It also stresses as a factor of weakness the disequilibrium between the modern and traditional sectors of the economy as well as between the North and the central and southern parts of the country.

There are four fundamental objectives set in the Perspective. The first is the "Tunisification" of the economy. Its aim is to reduce Tunisia's dependence upon France for exports and imports, and to decrease the foreign element in the financial, industrial, and agricultural sectors of the economy. The second goal is the *"promotion de l'homme,"* which is to be translated into equality of opportunity and the improvement of living standards; this involves a redistribution of income to provide better nourishment, housing, education, and health conditions for the mass of the people. The third is a reform of the basic structures of the economy; institutional reforms and investment are to remove the imbalance between different sections of the country and sectors of the economy. The last goal is self-development, the attainment of the stage of self-sustained growth, which will be reached when domestic savings are sufficient to cover gross investment requirements. According to the Perspective, this goal will be met by 1973.*

The Perspective establishes the following quantitative objectives to be reached by 1971.

1. Attain an annual rate of growth of 6 per cent and increase the gross domestic product to $1,157 million.

2. Increase domestic savings up to 26 per cent of the GDP by 1971.

3. Redistribute the national income to reach a minimum per capita income of 45 dinars ($107).

4. Attain a net investment for the 1962–71 period of 896 million dinars ($2,132 million), with investment by sectors as follows:

Infrastructure	$1,042 million
Agriculture	553 million
Industry	333 million
Education and Training of Technicians	183 million

Including allowances for maintenance of existing capital investment, the total gross investment required for the ten-year period is estimated at $2,800 million.[7]

A major problem confronting any country in the formulation

---

* The target set by the Perspective is a 6 per cent annual rate of growth, which would almost double the GDP in ten years (486 million dinars in 1972, as against 280 million in 1961). On the basis of a 4:1 capital-output ratio, considerable investment is needed to meet this target. Since the government has limited the contribution of foreign aid to 50 per cent of the net capital formation, domestic savings are supposed to increase from 11 per cent of GDP in 1962 to 20 per cent in 1965 and 26 per cent in 1971. Industrial production is to increase at the rate of more than 10 per cent a year; it will then represent 26 per cent of GDP. Agricultural production is to increase at the rate of 4 per cent a year; it will represent one-quarter of GDP in 1971, as against 30 per cent in 1962.

of a long-term economic plan is the establishment of a proper balance among the various objectives: overemphasis of a particular objective is usually at the expense of realizing other goals. The Tunisian Government is confronted with the problem of striking a balance between its concern for greater social justice, for full employment, and for an accelerated rate of growth.

One of the basic studies underlying the Perspective was a detailed social and economic survey of the fourteen governorates into which the country is divided. This study revealed that the governorates of Gabès, Gafsa, and Medenine, which form the whole southern portion of Tunisia and constitute half the land area of the country, have the lowest per capita income and are the least developed in terms of economic and social infrastructure. The governorates in the western and central parts of the country fare little better.

A major consideration of the Perspective is to increase investment in the South and Center, which comprise four-fifths of the country and 30 per cent of the population. Historically, investment has been concentrated in the North and in the eastern coastal region, with a steady migration of laborers up from the South. But from its inception, the Bourguiba Government has been responsive to the need of redressing the balance between the North and South, as well as between the modern and traditional sectors of the economy.

The poverty of the South is not the result of inhibiting social institutions or mores, but simply reflects the paucity of known resources in this area, which is either desert or semidesert, with an average yearly rainfall of about six inches. This area has limited investment opportunities and extremely low marginal productivity. Given Tunisia's limited domestic and foreign investment resources, and the great difference in productivity among the various sections of the country, it could be argued that it would be preferable to concentrate investment in the more productive North, which in turn could provide sufficient resources to help the South. Not only is a major breakthrough in agricultural production possible in the northern and coastal areas, but they already possess a substantial infrastructure of roads, railroads, ports, and electric power to support and service industry.

With regard to allocation of investment among the various sectors of the economy, a good case can be made for giving priority to agriculture over industry, for increasing and diversifying agricultural production and the processing of agricultural products. As in other underdeveloped countries, the agricultural sector must provide the initial increase in output needed to feed a steadily growing population and to generate the foreign exchange earnings needed for increased development in both industry and agriculture. An increased agricultural effort is the best way to raise the standard of living of the largest number of people, and thus expand the market for industrial goods. Fortunately, the agricultural sector of the Tunisian economy has great potential. A study of Tunisian agriculture undertaken by the Food and Agriculture Organization of the United Nations outlines the measures sufficient for increasing agricultural production by 50 per cent over the next ten years, and for providing 200,000 new jobs.[8] The Perspective, however, envisages a massive increase in the number of industrial workers, from 10 per cent of the active population in 1960 to 35 per cent in 1971, and a proportionate decrease of 300,000 jobs in the agricultural sector. As in other underdeveloped countries, rapid and massive industrialization is deemed essential for economic development, whatever the cost involved.

The importance of establishing investment priorities becomes more readily apparent if one considers the quantitative magnitude of the Perspective. It calls for an annual rate of growth of 6 per cent and for gross investment to average well over 20 per cent of the gross domestic product during the ten-year period. During the period 1950–53, the annual rate of growth was 5.6 per cent, with gross investment equal to almost 20 per cent of the GDP; but France was then making substantial investments in its Protectorate, largely in the modern sector of the economy, and primarily for the benefit of the *colons*. Compared to the performance of the Tunisian economy since independence, the projected rates of growth and levels of investment seem to be overambitious. Gross investment averaged $73 million for the period 1956 through 1960, whereas the Perspective requires it to average $280 million per year for the next decade. Either a reduction in targets or a stretch-out of the Plan period is likely to be required.

The Perspective assumes that 68 per cent of total gross investment requirements will come from domestic sources, and 32 per cent from foreign sources. In order to attain this goal, domestic savings are projected to increase to 26 per cent of the GDP by 1971, as compared to 7 per cent in 1961.[9] Since the Perspective envisages that the consumption of lower income groups will increase during the next decade, the bulk of the domestic savings will have to come from the higher income groups: Given the savings levels projected, confiscatory measures may be required. The other means envisaged to obtain adequate investment appear to be some collectivization in agriculture, and a large degree of Tunisification, or nationalization, of industry and commerce.

To this end, a law was passed on August 30, 1961, which stated that foreign firms must acquire Tunisian "nationality" at the end of one year's time: They must appoint a Tunisian president and have at least 50 per cent of the capital stock in Tunisian hands. Firms not complying with these conditions by the end of the stated period must either liquidate or obtain special authority from the Ministry of Plan and Finance to continue their operations. Exceptions to the law are banks, extractive industries, petroleum marketing and exploration firms, manufacturing companies, and companies operating under private or governmental agreement with the government of Tunisia. Although the exceptions would seem to be more important than the rule, the law may discourage potential foreign investors, who could regard it as the precursor of future nationalization.[10] Characteristically, the Tunisian Government, rather than relying upon private foreign investment, is actively negotiating for foreign public credits from both the West and the East.*

---

* The Three-Year Plan, covering the calendar years 1962–64, calls for a gross investment of $785 million, to be financed as follows: domestic savings to provide $416 million; U.S. long-term commitment, $180 million; non-U.S.

Concerning the Tunisification of agriculture, all the *colon* lands—some 1.5 million acres and 40 per cent of the agricultural output—are to be retrieved by 1964. The Perspective recognizes the danger of dividing large estates, since modern technology dictates that farms be large. It indicates that various types of cooperatives are contemplated, ranging from associations of individual landholders to collectives under state management.

In his speech of October 27, 1961, on "The Agricultural Aspect of the Economic Battle," Bourguiba made clear his concern for agricultural development, as well as his realistic approach to the problem. He pointed out that agriculture was the principal resource of Tunisia, and that increasing its production would benefit the great majority of the people. It was "a matter of life and death" to improve the quantity and quality of this production, which ruled out falling back on antiquated methods. It was necessary to maintain, he said, the level of production of the European settlers, which was a "positive aspect of colonization by which we must be inspired." Since the state could not develop directly all the lands restored to it, individual farmers would be allowed to lease these lands for a period of four years. In any case, there was no question of parceling and distributing the land, Bourguiba pointed out; for "what is important to me is the level of production." He went on to state his philosophy of planning:

> Our method is based on respect for the individual, not on class hatred or the dictatorship of the poor over the rich. Our sole guide is the

---

public assistance and foreign private investment, $165 million; and gold and foreign exchange reserves, $24 million. The promised contributions of West Germany, Italy, the U.S.S.R., Poland, Czechoslovakia, and Yugoslavia leave a small gap that France, it is hoped, will fill.

Dependence upon eventual foreign aid is made all the more necessary by the worsening of Tunisia's financial position in the last two years. A severe drought in 1960–61 has cut cereal production in half and reduced exports substantially. In 1961, the deficit of the current balance of payments was about $80 million and resulted in an $18 million drop in Tunisia's gold and foreign exchange reserve. The balance-of-payments deficit for 1962 is estimated at about $100 million, and the additional drain on reserves at $20 to $25 million. The pressure of unemployment also causes considerable strain on Tunisia's financial resources. With more than 200,000 people employed in the work camps, the cash wage payments and other operational costs of the program amount to about $30 million a year.

interest of the country, in which we are united for better or for worse. . . .

If the state, which is in a position to weigh the situation, decides on measures implying a restriction of a given freedom, the reconversion of a given crop, the redivision of certain agricultural lands, it is because it has been led to do so for imperative reasons of general interest.

In carrying out this gigantic task, using the method of Neo-Destourian Socialism, we are at the same time respecting the dignity of the individual. The latter must be convinced that the sacrifice he accepts, by agreeing to the restriction of some of his freedoms, is in his country's interest. He is not so different from a conscript who relinquishes his individual freedom when he is called up. He makes this sacrifice willingly.

Freely accepted discipline is the motive power of progress. We must realize this and fully familiarize ourselves with the idea that the individual's interest lies in the progress and well-being of the community.

The Three-Year Plan: 1962–64

Whereas the Perspective was intended to set goals and methods, the Three-Year Plan, launched early in 1962, sets detailed and concrete tasks for implementing these goals. It is significantly called a "pre-Plan," since one of its major roles is to provide experience for the subsequent Seven-Year Plan and to keep open the possibility of major changes in the light of new situations— such as a possible economic union of the Maghreb.

The targets are even more daring than those set by the Perspective. Agricultural production is to be raised 40 per cent above the average output in recent years. Industrial production, growing at the rate of 10 per cent a year, is to reach twice the production of 1957. The total national output is to increase by 39 per cent at the end of three years. This requires an investment effort one-third greater than the one foreseen in the Perspective; domestic savings are to rise from 10 per cent of the GDP in 1960 and 1961 to 20 per cent in 1964—probably an unrealistic goal. Also somewhat optimistic is the goal of total employment to be reached in 1964.

Yet, on the basis of actual performance, it is likely that the industrial sector will develop according to plan—despite a shortage of technical and managerial talent. This applies to the relatively large enterprises, mostly owned or controlled by the state, where the bulk of industrial investment has been directed. As for smaller and privately owned plants and businesses, it is open to question whether or not they will develop in large numbers—despite the incentives offered by the state. The problem here is one of attitudes conducive to risk-taking. Not only does the mobilization of savings tend to limit the scope of private investment, but the extensive price-control mechanisms established by the government may discourage would-be entrepreneurs who are now in the wholesale or retail trade and who feel hemmed in by governmental red tape.

In agriculture, the outlook is less promising in the short run, despite a major investment effort. Without ideal climatic conditions, the 40 per cent increase in production by 1964 is not likely to be reached. The Plan is based on the assumption that agricultural production can be increased at the same time as major institutional and structural changes are being introduced (i.e., the elimination of foreign farmers, the shifting of Tunisians from traditional subsistence to modern cash farming, the establishment of production cooperatives). The experience of the first year of the Plan indicates that the government is closer to meeting its goals where institutional changes are not involved than in those situations where such changes have been begun.

According to the Plan, the modern farms left by departing Europeans are to form nuclei around which traditional farmers will be organized on a cooperative basis so as to benefit from the machinery and the know-how of technicians in the modern farms. The main problem is the scarcity of administrators, engineers, technicians, extension workers, and maintenance men. The skilled personnel available to the Tunisian Government are only a fraction of the number now employed on *colon* farms. The dimension of the problem is indicated by the fact that the Perspective foresees the need for 884 agricultural engineers and 3,978 technicians during the ten-year period, whereas only 164 engineers and 461 technicians were available in 1961. It will take years before the graduates of the 15 new agricultural schools to be established are ready to step in. In the meantime, a possible decline of production on the modern farms may not be offset by a possible rise in the traditional sector.

In the long run, however, the Tunisian plans in agriculture seem sound. They include greater diversification in production, through the de-emphasis of wheat growing and the encouragement of fruit, vegetables, and livestock production. An intensive effort is being made to develop agricultural education at all levels. Various structures of production are being experimented with—from large exploitation units for cereal production in the North, which will be temporarily under state management, to various types of cooperatives for polyculture in the Center and South.

Although all the targets established by the Plan may not be reached in three years and although some of the Plan's aspects may be open to criticism, it is on the whole a serious program of development, carefully prepared, adjustable, and well understood and supported by the people. It justifies the amount of foreign aid Tunisia receives. If Tunisia receives more aid per capita than any other developing nation, this is a tribute to the soundness as well as to the scope of Tunisia's efforts at modernization.

If the Perspective and the Plan are to be judged not solely from economic criteria, but from a broader viewpoint, then their directives of self-help, social justice, and *"promotion de l'homme"* deserve high marks and could serve as a model for other countries. Their major shortcoming is that they are overly ambitious with regard to the rate of growth, investment, and domestic saving. But the Tunisians are realistic enough to have already reduced some of their targets—such as in housing.[11]

The Tunisian plans are not the product of doctrinaire ideology, but are essentially a pragmatic effort to reconcile equally valid goals, including the welfare and protection of the individual. The *"promotion de l'homme,"* the dignity and autonomy of the individual, have been basic preoccupations of the planners, who are aware of the dangers involved in collectivization and are opposed to its totalitarian implications. They are equally aware of the need to rely on the consent and participation of the people.

The most difficult task facing Tunisia in its economic effort is the selection of investment priorities, not only in terms of sectors, but also in terms of the type of investment. Does the fishing industry, for instance, need more boats or ports, or would a smaller investment in nets, lights, and technical training provide the same or even a greater increase in output? These analyses and decisions are much more difficult than drawing up the broad outlines of a plan for development.

The next major hurdle concerns practical managerial decisions at lower levels. Here the problem of training competent technicians and managers in adequate numbers is paramount. It may be questioned whether Tunisia can produce them soon enough for the rapid expansion of its economy—despite the government's emphasis on the maximum development of human resources.

Another major handicap is the small size of the Tunisian domestic market, which seems to preclude low-cost production of many manufactured goods. The Perspective assumes production for export by the projected industries, including those producing capital goods. But can these industries be competitive on world markets? Or is the long-term solution to enlarge Tunisian markets to include the whole of the Maghreb—itself linked to a larger economic unit, namely, the European community?

For a country with meager natural resources and a small market, the goal of self-sustained growth in the next ten years is probably unattainable. The price to pay for adequate growth may well be the creation of transnational institutions limiting national sovereignty.

Conclusion

From Tunisia's promising beginning as a new nation, it is possible to draw certain general conclusions. The first of these is the importance of timing in Tunisia's development. Despite the original asset of a relatively cohesive and settled society along the coast, Tunisia's story could have been quite different with a different sequence of events. We have noted the optimum impact of a colonial situation which started at the proper time and remained within bounds, the timely elimination of the Old Destour by its young rival, and the presence of a sizable intellectual elite who became the leaders and cadres of a modernizing movement. We have also noted the presence of a leader-hero who added competence and vision to charisma, and the long and constructive struggle of the Neo-Destour, which allowed Bourguiba to mold his party and the young generation to his image of the new Tunisia. Finally, the relatively late victory over the colonial power afforded enough time to prepare attitudes and skills for the challenge of independence, while the timely help of France, followed by that of the United States, gave the financial and economic support needed by the newly independent country.

A second important point is the primacy of politics over economics in the Tunisian pattern of modernization. Despite a large sector of traditional subsistence economy, low per capita income, and little industrialization, Tunisia has reached a high degree of political integration. There is no wide gap separating the small urban elite and the large traditionalist masses, as there is in most transitional societies. The party has had a broad popular base, and has succeeded in creating a near consensus on the goals and methods of modernization. The importance of the noneconomic factors in the process of modernization has been clearly demonstrated, from the emergence of the small aristocratic elite of Young Tunisians at the turn of the century to the formation of a broad political elite of Neo-Destourian cadres, the sons of the farmers of the Sahel as often as the sons of the bourgeois of Tunis. With this wide base, the party could success-fully mobilize the masses in the cities and countryside, first in the struggle for independence and later in the battle against underdevelopment.

Within this context of political mobilization, the prime im-portance of education stands out. The new political elite did not come from an economically or socially dominant class, but from the numerous graduates of French and Franco-Arab schools. The competition between the traditional Zitouna and the modern Western systems of education was decided in favor of the latter even before independence, thus sapping the strength of tradition and ensuring the victory of the modernist outlook. The Neo-Destour Party was and remains the major instrument of political education and social integration, spreading the modern ideology that President Bourguiba tirelessly expounds in his self-assumed role as tutor of his people. Formal education—modern, bilingual, and secular—will complete the process of transforming the out-look of the young generation and, typically, was given priority over the transformation of economic structures for years after independence. Institutional reforms, such as the new family code, are also aimed at transforming values and attitudes, as are the many organizations for men, women, and children at the local and national levels. Planning, carefully introduced by a massive educational campaign, is a vital element in the process of social integration begun some thirty years ago. It is social engineering par excellence, the mobilization of men's minds as well as of the country's resources.

Another generalization, somewhat linked to the preceding one, concerns the role of the one-party system, which, allowing a mini-mum of democracy at the beginning, in fact prepares the way for a more mature phase of democratic rule through the competition of organized political forces. Here the concept of consensus is essential to an understanding of the role that can be played by the single party in a transitional society. Agreement on basic values must be reached before a competition of parties can be safe and creative. Otherwise, the dialogue between traditionalists and modernists can only lead to an embittered and largely meaningless struggle, opening the way to demagogy and preventing the modern nation-state from being built on a foundation of active consent.

The problem for the new political oligarchy, of course, is to avoid abusing its power and to allow a relatively free expression of popular wishes and criticism. So far, the Neo-Destour leadership has shown that it knows how to exercise self-restraint and to apply the principles of its liberal philosophy. It has taken seriously its function of teaching the people political maturity and responsibility. It remains to be seen, however, whether the cult of the leader will dissolve the ethical foundations of the political system, and whether the imperatives of economic planning will lead to the adoption of totalitarian short cuts. It remains to be seen, also, whether the new political elite will be able to function effectively without its prestigious leader.

A final generalization must be made about the conflict inherent in the process of building a modern nation-state. Is the emphasis to be put on total independence or on successful modernization? Until 1961, it appeared that the Tunisians had opted for the latter, even at the cost of accepting limitations to their sovereignty through continued ties with France. But 1961, the "year of the Plan," was also the year of Bizerte, and it may have marked the beginning of a new era of nationalist self-assertion.

On the other hand, the pragmatic quality of the Tunisians may well lead them to realize the limitations of formal independence for a weak and exposed country, as well as the fact that its limited resources preclude a rapid economic development without massive foreign aid for an indeterminate period. If successful modernization continues to be the primary goal, perhaps a limitation of national sovereignty within a Maghrebin context will not be considered too heavy a price to pay. By generating self-confidence, the consolidation of the nation-state and the present mobilization of energies and resources may make it easier for Tunisians to accept transnational ties within a larger unit. For the main assets of Tunisia—social and political cohesion and creative efforts at modernization—compensate somewhat for its handicaps in size and resources, and may allow the little country to initiate the type of policy that would give North Africa both the substance of independence and a reasonable guarantee of economic prosperity. For better or for worse, the future of Tunisia is linked with the destiny of the Maghreb as a whole. That it may help shape this destiny is somewhat reassuring.

It is the quality of balanced and wise experimentation that has differentiated Tunisia's process of modernization from those of other Arab countries and that has prompted U.S. financial backing of its ambitious Ten-Year Plan. This favored treatment is due not so much to Bourguiba's long-lasting pro-Western stand as to the recognition of the Tunisians' hard work, integrity, and seriousness of purpose, qualities often lacking in countries better endowed by nature.

Another reason for this special recognition is the fact that Tunisia—which prides itself on its historical role as a natural bridge between Eastern and Western Mediterranean lands—is soberly attempting, in addition to its economic development, a cultural and political synthesis that may prove a model for other developing nations. Bourguiba's continued attempt to make his country a meeting ground for African spokesmen, while keeping friendly ties with the West and an open mind about the East, is indicative of the positive role Tunisia can play on the unpredictable African scene.

Notes

Notes

1. Edward Shils, "Further Observations on Mrs. Huxley," *Encounter*, October, 1961, p. 45.

PART I. STAGES IN THE PROCESS OF CHANGE

Chapter 2. The First Stage: Early Western Impact
(pp. 7–21)

1. These quotations are taken from Paul Lapie, *Les Civilisations Tunisiennes*, Paris, 1898. A teacher of philosophy at Lycée Carnot in Tunis, Lapie makes an interesting attempt to formulate sociological rules for the different mentalities of the three communities in Tunisia—Moslem, Jewish, and European Christian. Traces of his influence are found in later articles and books by Tunisians.

2. Daniel Grasset, "L'Instruction Publique en Tunisie," *Revue Africaine*, 1878, pp. 183–201.

3. As stated by French Premier Waldeck-Rousseau.

4. Written under the pseudonym "P. N. X." (d'Estournelles de Constant), *La Politique française en Tunisie, le protectorat et ses origines: 1854–1891* (Paris, 1891), p. 459.

5. See Sheik Mohammed El Fadl Ben Achour, *Al Haraka al Adabiya wa al Fikriya fi Tunis (The Literary and Intellectual Movement in Tunisia)* (Cairo, 1956), pp. 43–44.

6. There had been an earlier official newspaper, *Al Ra'id*, dating back to 1860, which had been revived by Kheireddine and used as a mouthpiece for his reformist views.

7. Ben Achour, *op. cit.*, p. 54.

8. Cf. Mohammed Lasram, "Une Association en Tunisie—la Khaldouniya" (report presented to the 1906 Congrès Colonial de Marseille) (Tunis, 1906); reprinted in *Le Tunisien*, August 27, 1908.

Chapter 3. Stage Two: The Young Tunisians, or, The Age of Reason
(pp. 22–37)

1. *Le Tunisien*, February 7, 1907.

2. *Ibid.*

3. *Ibid.*, October 27, 1910. The author was Ahmed Essafi, later a leader in the Old Destour Party.

4. *Ibid.*, December 18, 1908.

5. *Ibid.,* December 30, 1909.
6. *Ibid.,* October 20, 1910.
7. *Ibid.,* January 5, 1911.
8. Cf. Lasram, *op. cit.*
9. *Le Tunisien,* January 28, 1909. Note also the motion of indigenous delegates to the Consultative Conference reported in *Le Tunisien,* December 5, 1907.
10. *Ibid.,* February 11, 1909.
11. *Ibid.* (Italics in original.)
12. This information, based on a brief article by Khairallah ben Mustafa in *Al Majallah al Zitouniya (Zitouna University Journal)* (Tunis), March, 1939, also buttresses the argument that the Young Tunisians usually undertook private schemes more to stimulate state action than as a substitute for state action.
13. Khairallah ben Mustafa, "L'Enseignement Primaire des Indigènes en Tunisie," *Congrès de l'Afrique du Nord tenu à Paris du 6 au 10 Octobre 1908 compte rendu des travaux* (Proceedings of the Congrès de l'Afrique du Nord) (Paris, 1909).
14. *Le Tunisien,* February 25, 1909.
15. *Ibid.,* November 5, 1908.
16. *Ibid.,* April 18, 1907.

Chapter 4. Stage Three: The Era of the Old Destour
(pp. 38–66)

1. M. Barthélemy and M. Weiss, who so advised in 1921.
2. *La Tunisie Martyre* (Paris, 1920), p. 47.
3. *L'Esprit Libéral du Coran* (Paris, 1905), p. 88.
4. Mohamed Saleh Mzali, *L'Evolution Economique de la Tunisie* (Tunis, 1921), p. 7. Mzali's eventual fate was unfortunate. Inexplicably, he agreed to serve as Prime Minister in March, 1954, when the French Government was making a final attempt to destroy the Tunisian nationalist movement on the one hand, while granting certain internal reforms on the other. As a result, he was sentenced to ten years' imprisonment by the special Haute Cour set up after independence.
5. *Ibid.,* p. 57.
6. *La Tunisie Martyre,* pp. 199–200.
7. Haddad, *Al Ummal al Tunisiyun wa zuhur al Haraka al Naqabiya* (Tunis, 1925).
8. Haddad, *Imra'atina fi al Shari'a wa al Mujtama'* (Tunis, 1930).
9. *Al Ummal al Tunisiyun* . . . , p. 15.
10. *Ibid.,* p. 14.
11. Cf. Elie Cohen-Hadria, *Du Protectorat Français à l'Indépendence Tunisienne—Souvenirs d'un Témoin Socialiste* (MSS, dated 1959–60), p. 54.
12. *Tunis Socialiste,* September 3, 1924.
13. *Ibid.,* March 31, 1925.
14. *Al Ummal al Tunisiyun* . . . , pp. 124–25.
15. *Ibid.,* p. 129. "Setting one's own house in order" was a theme of many of Bourguiba's speeches and writings, beginning just a few years later.

16. *Ibid.*, p. 123.
17. *Ibid.*, p. 48.
18. Ben Achour, *op. cit.*, p. 62.
19. *L'Etendard Tunisien*, May 11, 1929. This newspaper, edited by Chedhli Khairallah, had as its contributors the leading thinkers of the later Neo-Destour including Bourguiba, Tahar Sfar, and Bahri Guiga. This unsigned article was the work of Khairallah.
20. R. P. Andre Demeerseman, *Confession d'un Musulman* (MSS in Tunis), pp. 121–22.
21. *L'Etendard Tunisien*, December 6 and 27, 1929.
22. *L'Action Tunisienne*, April 21, 1933.
23. *Ibid.*, April 14, 1933.
24. "Issus des couches populaires les plus humbles—et c'est là notre orgueil . . . ," Mohammed Bourguiba in *L'Action Tunisienne*, November 3, 1932.
25. Cf. the articles by Ali Bu Hajib entitled "Voix du Guenillard," in *L'Action Tunisienne*.
26. *Le Libéral*, February 7, 1925.
27. Bahri Guiga, in *L'Action Tunisienne*, January 13, 1933.
28. *L'Etendard Tunisien*, January 11, 1929.
29. *Ibid.*, February 1, 1929.
30. *Koran*, 2:186.
31. *Ibid.*, 2:287.
32. *Ibid.*, 6:165, and also 53:39. (Literally, "No burden-bearer shall bear the burden of another.")
33. Quoted in Habib Bourguiba, *La Tunisie et La France* (Paris, 1954), pp. 73–74.
34. Ali Belhaouan, *Tunis al Tha'ira* (*Revolutionary Tunisia*) (Cairo, 1954), p. 46.
35. From the Introduction to Bourguiba's *La Tunisie et La France* (in which the editors describe the Bourguiba political method), p. 12.
36. *Ibid.*

PART II. THE ERA OF THE NEO-DESTOUR

Chapter 2. The Political Background
(pp. 73–88)

1. Speech on June 1, 1959, to the Tunisian Constituent Assembly.
2. *Voix du Tunisien*, April 10, 1931.
3. Speech on June 24, 1961.
4. Bourguiba, *op. cit.*, p. 256.
5. Speech on April 6, 1961.
6. Bourguiba, *op. cit.*, p. 171.
7. Bourguiba's opening address to the Sixth National Congress of the Neo-Destour Party, March 2, 1959.
8. Hedi Nouira, "Le Neo-Destour," *Politique Etrangère*, XIX, No. 3 (July, 1954), p. 317.
9. Speech on November 7, 1958.

Chapter 3. Nation-Building
(pp. 89–110)

1. *Esprit* (Paris), June, 1957, p. 891.
2. Speech on August 8, 1957.
3. As Bourguiba described the main requirements of leadership in a letter to a favorite subordinate in 1952. See *La Tunisie et la France*, pp. 375–78.
4. Speech on December 27, 1956.
5. Speech on December 5, 1957.
6. Speech on October 2, 1958.
7. *Petit Matin* (Tunis), April 10, 1959.
8. Speech on March 30, 1961.

Chapter 4. How Much Democracy?
(pp. 111–128)

1. *L'Action*, January 7, 1957.
2. Speech reported in *Petit Matin*, January 20, 1957.
3. *L'Action*, February 4, 1957.
4. *Ibid.*, October 14, 1957.
5. *Ibid.*, May 26, 1958.
6. *Ibid.*, July 7, 1958.
7. *Ibid.*, September 8, 1958.
8. Communiqué of the Political Bureau, September 8, 1958.
9. *Afrique-Action*, October 7, 1961.
10. See *Petit Matin*, November 1–5, 1961, for full French translations of the editorials.
11. *Es Sabah*, November 15, 1961.
12. *Afrique-Action*, November 7–13, 1961.

PART III. SOCIAL AND ECONOMIC CHANGE

Chapter 1. A Strategy of Modernization?
(pp. 131–139)

1. As quoted in Moncef Guen, *La Tunisie Indépendante face à son Economie* (Tunis, 1961), p. 184.
2. *Ibid.*, p. 47.
3. *Ibid.*, p. 184.
4. *Ibid.*, p. 180. See also Habib Bourguiba's speech "Explanations and Clarification," November 18, 1961.
5. Gabriel Ardant, *La Tunisie d'Aujourd'hui et de Demain* (Paris, 1961), pp. 39 ff. For a Marxist interpretation of the impact of French colonialism see Paul Sebag, *La Tunisie, essai de Monographie* (Paris, 1951).
6. This process is well described in "Vieilles Familles et Nouvelle Elite en Tunisie," an unpublished study by Henri de Montéty.

Chapter 2. Social Change: Clearing the Way to Progress
(pp. 140–167)

1. *Building a New Tunisia: Comments on an Address by Habib Bourguiba* (American Universities Field Staff: Reports Service, North African Series, VII, No. 1), p. 6.

2. The best treatment of the situation of women in Tunisia is Henri de Montéty's *Femmes de Tunisie* (Paris, 1950). See also his "Mutation des moeurs familiales en Tunisie," in *Cahiers Nord-Africains*, No. 77 ("Visages de la Tunisie, 1960"), pp. 18–27.

3. For a brief treatment of the new Code, see J. M. Verdier, "Le nouveau droit de la famille en Tunisie," in *Cahiers Nord-Africains*, No. 77, pp. 13–17.

4. Michel Lelong, "L'enseignement tunisien en 1959," in *Cahiers Nord-Africains*, No. 77, pp. 28–31.

5. For this and the following information see the brochure *Perspective Décennale de Scolarisation 1959–1968* (Secretariat of State for National Education [Tunis, 1959]). *La Presse* of August 12, 1962, states that 25.38 per cent of the total budget was devoted to education in 1961–62, of which 22.84 per cent went to the Ministry of National Education.

6. *Perspective Décennale. . . .* See also *Nouvelle Conception de l'Enseignement en Tunisie* (Secretariat of State for National Education [Tunis, October, 1958]).

7. Quoted by Leon Carl Brown in "Education, Cultural Unity and the Future," newsletter of December 1, 1960, to the Institute of Current World Affairs.

8. In a press conference held on September 29, 1962, Mr. Messadi reiterated that Arabic would replace French as soon as enough teachers were available. He added that French would always hold a privileged position since it would continue to be taught for ten school years—four years in primary school and throughout secondary school (*La Presse*, September 30, 1962).

9. In the press conference cited above, Mr. Messadi gave the following enrollment figures: 481,483 students in primary schools (77.68 per cent of all school-age boys and 36.68 per cent of school-age girls); 14,055 students in intermediate schools, and 37,223 in secondary schools during the academic year 1961–62. The figure of 5,269 university students (including 2,500 in foreign universities) appears in *La Presse*, August 12, 1961.

10. *Study of the Creation of the Tunisian University* (Secretariat of State for National Education [Tunis, 1960]).

11. *Situation Scolaire trois premières années de l'application du plan décennal de scolarisation* (Secretariat of State for National Education, June, 1961).

12. République Tunisienne, *Perspective Décennale de Développement, 1962–1971*, p. 342.

13. Ardant, *op. cit.*, p. 56.

14. For this and following information, see *Nouveau Régime Foncier en Tunisie* (Etudes et Documents [Secretariat of State for Information], Series A, No. 2, June 15, 1959).

15. Mahmoud Tarzi, "Une première loi agraire en Tunisie," in *Aspects et Perspectives économiques de la Tunisie*, No. 2, March, 1959. See also "La mise en valeur de la Vallée de la Medjerda" (Secretariat of State for Information [Tunis, 1959]).

Chapter 3. Economic Change: From Pragmatism to Plan
(pp. 168–186)

1. For the background of the Tunisian economy, see Moncef Guen, *op.*

cit.; Report on Tunisia (Food and Agriculture Organization of the United Nations, Mediterranean Development Project [Rome, 1959]); and the brochures of the Secretariat of State for Information, "Tunisia Works" and "Perspectives Tunisiennes 1962–1971."

2. For the figures on gross domestic product and gross investment between 1950 and 1959 see *La Situation Economique à la fin de 1959* (République Tunisienne, Service des Statistiques), pp. 42–45. See also the United Nations *Yearbook of National Accounts Statistics 1960*, p. 268.

3. For the revenues and expenditures in the Tunisian budget from 1955 through 1960 see the Banque Centrale de Tunisie, *Rapport annuel 1959*, pp. 41–43, and the *Rapport annuel 1960*, pp. 31–32.

4. Banque Centrale de Tunisie, *Bulletin*, No. 8, January, 1961, p. 8; also International Monetary Fund, *International Financial Statistics*, XIV, October, 1961, 20–21. On December 31, 1961, Tunisia's gold and foreign exchange reserves totaled $78.8 million, as compared with $97 million at the end of 1960. (Chemical Bank New York Trust Company, *International Economic Survey*, No. 136, June, 1962.)

5. *La Dépêche Tunisienne*, November 9, 1960.

6. *Rapport annuel 1960*, p. 29. Through June 30, 1961, the U.S. Government had provided over 250,000 metric tons of wheat valued at about $17 million at world market price. The wage payments for 160,000 workers cost the Tunisian Government about $18.5 million per year and represented a substantial burden on its limited financial resources. Total U.S. aid to Tunisia—economic and technical assistance, agricultural commodities and Development Loan Fund—amounted to $227.9 million from July, 1957, through June, 1961.

7. *Perspective Décennale de Développement, 1962–1971*, p. 60. All statistics in the Perspective are calculated at constant 1957 prices. The GDP for 1961 was estimated at $646 million.

8. *Report on Tunisia*, pp. 147–56.

9. Even more significant than the increase of domestic savings in relation to GDP are the yearly increases in domestic savings required: 70 per cent in 1962, 45 per cent in 1963, and 20 per cent in 1964 and in 1965.

10. The law of August 30, 1961, has only partially been implemented. French businessmen are allowed to continue their operations as formerly—under the supervision of various government offices.

11. It had been envisaged in the Perspective that almost 25 per cent ($545 million) of the net investment during the period 1962–71 would be allocated to housing—a proportion that was later sharply reduced.

Index

Index

DATE DUE
